AFRICAN MADNESS

AFRICAN

MADNESS

Alex Shoumatoff

ALFRED A. KNOPF   NEW YORK   1988

THIS IS A BORZOI BOOK

PUBLISHED BY ALFRED A. KNOPF, INC.

"The Woman Who Loved Gorillas" ("The Fatal Obsession of
Dian Fossey"), "The Emperor Who Ate His People" ("Fall of
a Savage Emperor"), and "In Search of the Source of AIDS"
were originally published in somewhat different form in *Vanity
Fair*.

"The Last of the Dog-Headed Men" ("Look at That") was originally published in somewhat different form in *The New Yorker*.

Library of Congress Cataloging-in-Publication Data

Shoumatoff, Alex.
African madness.

1. Africa, Sub-Saharan—Description and travel—
1981–   . 2. Shoumatoff, Alex—Journeys—Africa,
Sub-Saharan. 3. Fossey, Dian. 4. Bokassa I, Emperor
of the Central African Empire, 1921–   .
5. AIDS (Disease)—Africa, Sub-Saharan. I. Title.
DT352.2.S48   1988   967'.0328   88-45345
ISBN 0-394-56914-8

Manufactured in the United States of America
First Edition

For Sharon Delano, who gets involved,
and my late agent, Luis Sanjurjo,
who knew everybody yet
remained an enigma to all of us

I believe one has to abandon the idea of global, massive progress that is valid for all societies. I think one can speak of progress with a little "p," and in the plural. In certain epochs in certain places of the earth certain progresses have occurred, which have probably been paid for with regression in other domains.

Claude Lévi-Strauss

On n'est plus chez soi, assis sur la tradition. On est dans le monde entier.

Benoit Quersin

CONTENTS

Preface xi

The Woman Who Loved Gorillas 3

The Last of the Dog-Headed Men 43

The Emperor Who Ate His People 91

In Search of the Source of AIDS 129

PREFACE

In 1986 and 1987 I took four trips to Africa. I had by then been making periodic visits to the tropics for fifteen years or so, going down once or twice a year for a month or two or six or eight. I started out going to Jamaica, then I got deeply into Brazil. In 1981 I went to Zaire for two months, and there, as a Belgian friend who has lived in Kinshasa for twenty years describes the process, I caught *la microbe*: Africa got into my blood. (This was before the AIDS virus was identified and spoiled his metaphor.)

My vision of the tropics was, and still is, largely romantic. I was, and am, swept away by these worlds of ecstatic light and color and overpowering beauty, by the birds, flowers, and butterflies, by the seething, radiant life of the rain forests and the markets, by the generosity and the gentleness of the people, by the music and the slow, delicious rhythm of life. Canoeing up some jungle river, leaving the Third World behind and entering the Fourth or Fifth, the time of Daniel Boone, of hearty pioneer families living in the middle of nowhere off what they could grow, gather, fish, or hunt; proceeding beyond them back into the Neolithic, to villages where people lived close to the way humans have lived for most of their history, I felt alive and engaged in a way I had never felt in my world. I came to need these trips to get my juices flowing again and to recover the sense of wonder, so hard to sustain in these cynical times.

But the more of these trips I took, the more I became aware of the deep, chronic problems of the equatorial zones, of what Claude Lévi-Strauss has called the *tristes tropiques*, and the more, indeed, the problems themselves were intensifying. It was my luck to have come upon these places at a time when they were undergoing biological and cultural destruction on an unprecedented scale, due to overpopulation and the arrival of modern inventions like bulldozers, chain saws, defoliants, and television. I could not help becoming aware of the political and economic bind they were in. Owing the greater part of their gross national product to Western creditors, they were invariably run by ruthless strongmen and elites whose only interest was in keeping things as they were. Inevitably the flip side of the tropical paradise became more apparent. During the seventies I saw Jamaica turn from a bright, sunny island to a dark, dangerous one, full of looting and shooting. As millions of young people with no chances came of age, a similiar wave of violence spread over Brazil in the eighties. In April, 1987, two young masked gunmen from a nearby *favela*, or shantytown, broke into a beach house up the coast from Rio where we were spending the weekend. Learning that I was American, one of them put his gun to my head, and it was only the quick thinking of my Brazilian wife, who showed him our children asleep in the next room, that kept him from pulling the trigger. If I had been closing my eyes to certain things I hadn't wanted to see, they were now fully open.

It was in this context—the tropics were disintegrating, and my vision of them was growing darker—that my last four trips to Africa were taken. The murder of Dian Fossey focused one of the continent's most pressing problems: the need to protect what is left of its magnificent flora and fauna versus the need of its exploding local populations for more space to live and grow food in—twenty-three thousand new families in tiny Rwanda need land each year. To me the Batwa Pygmies, the original inhabitants of Central Africa, are as endangered and as deserving of protection as the gorillas themselves. They have been hunters from time immemorial and are now forbidden to hunt in the Virungas, the last patch of forest left in Rwanda, because gorillas sometimes step into their antelope snares. When I learned that Dian had tortured Pygmies brought to her by her antipoaching patrols, I wondered what sort of a person she was, or had become. She arrived in Africa a fairly typical specimen of the American middle class. Due to an eccentric theory of Louis Leakey she was placed in an extraordinary situation—alone on a mountain in the middle of Africa with several hundred gorillas facing imminent annihilation, and although she was completely out of her element, she was determined not to let them down. By the end of the seventies, the isolation, the struggle against a multitude of enemies, real and imagined, and a number of terrible things that happened to her became more than she could deal with. The decapitation of her beloved Digit finally pushed her over the edge. She snapped. I was amazed to learn that there were so many suspects in her murder. She had alienated so many people that even after her death a vortex of violence and madness seemed to swirl around her camp.

A few months later I returned to the African region on a happier mission: realizing a longstanding dream, I finally got to Madagascar. It was the first time my two boys had been in a rain forest. We found singular plants and animals and cheerful people living in vast extended families whose dead members, "the ancestors," sometimes inhabiting a venerable tree or rock or taking the form of a butterfly, a boa, a crocodile, or a lemur, continue to play a vital role in their daily affairs. The piece is a tropical eclogue, a celebration of a lost, enchanted island world that is on the verge of being obliterated. Eighty percent of the Malagasy are farmers and their need for more land is perhaps even more desperate than that of the Banyarwanda; as Alison and Richard Jolly write, they are being forced to play out a "tragedy without villains," to sacrifice their future in order to survive in the present. But we were carefully shielded from all unpleasantness. Roger Rakotomala, who runs a San Francisco-based outfit called Lemur Tours and who set up our trip, had gone ahead to make sure that everything was "superlative," and it was. The only madness we found on Madagascar was in the country's first syllable. A few weeks after we left, however, there was an eruption of angry madness: all over the island the Malagasy rose up and assaulted the Indian shopkeepers. The Indians are a favorite target in Africa when things are going badly.

From an overloaded, nostalgic Western perspective, traditional African village life, such as we found on Madagascar, may seem idyllic, but it, too, has drawbacks, especially for the women, who grow old quickly, working from dawn to dusk for their in-laws, hauling firewood and water, digging in the fields. The general level of paranoia in the villages is high. One is afraid of being persecuted by the ghosts of the dead, of being bewitched by one's enemies, and of being accused of witchcraft oneself. But as a way of life the villages are stable and comprehensible, and almost oppressively sane. Everyone is a known quantity, and everyone is taken care of.

It is only when large cities begin to appear in the landscape, as they did in the seventies, when eleven cities in Central Africa grew to have populations of more than a million, that a societal madness begins to occur; that detribalized young men, lost souls wandering in the vast space between the traditional and the modern worlds, can be heard howling in the streets of downtown Nairobi in the middle of the night; that stark naked *aliénés* can be seen rummaging in the ditches of Bangui. In several Central African cities I have heard the same piercing, ululating cry, like the falsetto whoop of an Indian tamping his mouth with his hand. Different tribes have different ways of taking it. In the church of Notre Dame de Fatima in Kinshasa, it was emitted by an oversouling Bakongo woman as a *cri de joie*. The Balunda also traditionally make this cry, during coronation festivities, for instance; so do the Baganda. In these tribes it means happiness. But to the Tutsi—the famous Watusis—it means help, danger, as when a burglar is breaking in. It is also the sound that mad people make, "no one knows why," a Ugandan woman told me. I had heard it in the streets of Nairobi and outside a hospital in Kampala, she explained, because "most of the people who run mad in the villages move to the towns, I think because there are more things for them to do."

Only with the trauma of colonization, followed by sudden decolonization, when collections of tribes, some of them traditional enemies, are left on their own, to embark on shaky and perhaps inappropriate experiments in nation-statehood, does one find the major lunacy of an Idi Amin or a Jean-Bédel Bokassa. These *grands monstres* were products of a certain time that, one hopes, has been put behind; they stepped into a vacuum, and there was no one to curb their excesses. "Bokassa was stupid and alcoholic but he was not a bad man," an expatriate who claimed to have eaten human flesh with him in one of his palaces told me; he was just living out the fantasies of a tribal chief, to have any woman he wanted, to have his cup refilled with Chivas as soon as it was empty. The evidence of Bokassa's cannibalism is anecdotal, but it comes from many sources and is strengthened by the revelation in Poutrin's turn-of-the-century ethnography that his tribe, the M'Baka, has a tradition of cannibalism. I have no trouble believing that the emperor served *entrecôtes* of subjects who had fallen into disfavor to his guests.

While I was in Bangui my literary agent, Luis Sanjurjo, died. We had known each other since college in the late sixties, having moved on different peripheries of the same crowd. Luis

had been my agent for seven years. Things were finally starting
to click: he put me together with Sharon Delano, one of the most
brilliant and exacting magazine editors in New York, and Sharon
did wonders with the Fossey piece, which Luis later sold to
Hollywood for big bucks. But that fall a malignant lymphoma
the size of a golf ball was removed from his neck. We all thought
he had the cancer licked but a few months later it returned.
Under massive daily doses of radio- and chemotherapy he went
down fast. I spoke with him the day before I flew to Bangui.
His discourse was rambling, but he still managed to come up
with shrewd advice for my latest career crisis. A few days later
he was dead of pneumonia. He insisted on there being no autopsy
and denied to the end that he had AIDS but the profile was
classic. The lymphoma was Burkitt's, the pneumonia was his
second bout with *Pneumocystis carinii* (PCP). He was gay, and
quite a number of his Fire Island friends had already or have
since succumbed to the disease. I still remember his phone
number: 556-5652. It was a lifeline for me and his other clients.
I can still hear his famous words of encouragement: "Well *done.*"

So there was no question that when Sharon asked me if I
would do a piece on AIDS in Africa, I had to go. I felt I owed
it to Luis to try to get to the bottom of this horrible waster of
life in its prime. It was also the biggest story in Africa, yet
nobody seemed to have told it. My swing through four countries
in the AIDS belt proved to be the grimmest, most ungluing
month I have ever spent. In Guinea-Bissau, a fascinating place,
one of the last countries in Africa, or anywhere, that hasn't been
sucked into the modern orbit, about half a dozen cases a week
of the apparently slower-spreading and -acting virus, HIV-2,
are going into the main hospital in the capital. It remains to be
seen whether they are just the unfortunate few who have been
singled out by the disease or represent the beginning of a massive

epidemic. In southern Uganda an epidemic of HIV-1 AIDS is raging out of control. Whole villages on the Tanzanian border are being wiped out. It is like the plague, a living nightmare of the Apocalypse. And this on top of the incessant civil unrest that the Ugandans have had to endure since independence, one army after another marching over the landscape, "all those young men with needs to be taken care of," as a Ugandan health official put it. I had never seen lives being snuffed out like this before. The majority of Ugandans seemed to accept this calamity, only the latest in a series that has beset them since independence, but certainly the most horrible one of all, the final flail, with an equanimity that to me was incomprehensible and which I realized must be the product of an utterly un-Western attitude toward death and the self and the purpose of living. The suicides— people in the early stages of the disease hanging or electrocuting themselves or swallowing rat poison rather than wasting to death over a period of several months or years—were easier to understand.

This was not what I wanted out of Africa at all. I wanted to revel in the wild and the primitive, to spend time with the people and groove on the scenery, but instead I was compelled to document the disintegration of beautiful young men and women, of the very fabric of African society, to which sex and a pervasive sensuality in all dealings are central. And the worst of it is the absolute hopelessness of the situation. There is no cure in sight. Millions of Africans are going to die, and nothing can be done about it.

At this point none of the basic questions—when, where, how, or why the virus or viruses broke out, how many viruses there are, how many are infected, whether all of them will die, whether HIV acts alone or with cofactors—has been answered. The picture is still growing more confused than clearer. By the time this book is in the reader's hands, more of the picture will undoubtedly have been fleshed out, and some of the information and speculation presented here will almost certainly be out of date. The piece is intended, therefore, for the historical record.

Mexico City
March, 1988

AFRICAN MADNESS

THE WOMAN
WHO LOVED
GORILLAS

The rains in Rwanda had let up that December when Dian Fossey was murdered in her cabin in the mountains, but by the time I arrived, a few months later, they were coming down hard, twice a day. The airport at Kigali, the capital, was socked in. Through the clouds I caught glimpses of long ridges and deep valleys terraced with rows of bananas, beans, sweet potatoes. Rwanda is one of the smallest, poorest, and most densely populated countries in Africa. There are 5.9 million Banyarwanda, as the people are called—more than 500 per square mile. Almost every available patch of land is under cultivation, and 23,000 new families need land each year. Women do most of the farming—black Bahutu women in bold-patterned sarongs who look up from black furrows of rich volcanic soil and give you thousand-dollar smiles. Rwanda feeds itself, and though it is poor it is at peace, and because it is at peace, and is in the Western camp and surrounded by large, uncoalesced countries where anything could happen—Zaire, Uganda, Tanzania—it gets a lot of aid. The Banyarwanda, who Dian called "woggiepoos," are hardworking, amiable, courteous, easygoing, and quite prudish. Their president, Général-Major Juvénal Habyarimana, who came to power in a coup fifteen years ago, is a model of moderation. The main roads, recently paved by the Chinese, are in great shape. Radio communications are excellent; if you want to get hold of someone, you just send a message on the radio. The civil servants are at their desks, and they are paid on time. If Africa is Oz, an Africanist in New York told me, Rwanda is the Land of the Munchkins.

The center of excitement for expatriates in Kigali is the Hôtel des Mille Collines, with its pool and lavish buffet. This was where Dian stayed when she came down from the mountain for a little R and R, put on a smashing dress she had bought on one of her shopping sprees in London, and went partying with her embassy friends. Sooner or later every *mzungu* (the Central African term for white person) in Rwanda you are looking for is bound to show up at the Mille Collines.

Within hours of checking in I ran into David Watts, who had just arrived to take over Dian's job as director of the Karisoke Research Center—the station for the study of mountain gorillas that she had set up and continued to run for the better part of two decades. David is thirty-five, single, with round wire-rimmed glasses and graying hair parted in the middle, a jacket and tie and backpack—a refined, thoughtful individual who looks as though he might play the violin, which he in fact does. He had spent a total of about two years during the late seventies on the mountain with Dian. They had not parted friends. In the last few days he had been making it clear to the Rwandan authorities that he was eager to play ball with them—something Dian had been singularly uninterested in doing. The gorillas around Karisoke have become very important to the Rwandan economy. They are the fourth largest source of foreign exchange for the country; about six thousand tourists a year, at sixty dollars a head, go up the mountain to see them. The tourists also stay in hotels, rent cars, eat, and buy things.

A few days after meeting David at the Mille Collines, I went to visit the gorillas with three other Americans. Our guide

led us through fields planted with a daisylike flower called pyrethrum, from which a biodegradable insecticide is made. In
1969, about forty percent of the forest in the Parc des Volcans,
where most of the gorillas live, was cleared and planted with
pyrethrum for export to the West, but even before the first crop
was harvested, cheaper, synthetic insecticides had been developed, and the bottom fell out of the pyrethrum market. That the
gorillas' habitat was decimated so that we Westerners, while
dumping our hazardous insecticides on the Third World, could
have a safe insecticide we didn't even want after all is typical
of the ironies of Third World conservation. Just as it was the
West, so concerned with saving the gorillas, that provided the
outlets for gorilla poaching: until four or five years ago, when
public outcry pretty much put a stop to the mountain-gorilla
market, wildlife traffickers could get a couple of hundred thousand dollars for one in good condition. Physical anthropology
departments at universities were eager to acquire their skeletons
or skulls and thoughtless tourists brought back hands as me-
mentos of their trips to Africa.

The gorillas we were looking for hang out in the bamboo
forest and the nettle meadows on the lower slopes of Mount
Visoke. We caught up with them some twenty minutes from
where they had been left the day before. There were twelve of
them—Ndume, the silverback, his three mates, and eight young
ones. They were making their way down a hillside, eating stinging nettle and wild celery as they went. Ndume weighs about
three hundred pounds and eats about forty pounds of vegetation
a day. He had lost his right hand in a poacher's snare. We sat
down fifteen feet from him and waited to see what happened.
Our guide had said to make no sudden moves, and if charged
to hit the dirt. Ndume knuckle-walked to within two feet of me
and sat down, facing the other way, completely ignoring us. His
head, with its massive brow ridge and powerful jaws, was huge.

After fifteen minutes he ambled over to a comfortable-looking spot and, snorting contentedly, proceeded to sack out. There he remained, dead to the world, limbs akimbo, until we left. The other gorillas circled around us curiously. Safari walked out to the edge of a branch and jumped up and down on it. The branch snapped and she came tumbling down into a thicket and dropped from sight. Kosa, the subdominant male, reached up to a shrub and pulled it toward his mouth, releasing hundreds of fluffy seeds into the air. An unnamed young female walked toward us, briskly beating her chest for a few seconds (it was more like fluttering than pounding, and seemed to be meant more in friendship than intimidation), sat down beside me, put my poncho in her mouth, bashed me on the knee a couple of times, and then went over to her mother. I tried to catch a glint of recognition in the gorillas' soft brown eyes, but they remained glossed over, wild. It was clear, though, that they trusted us, maybe more than they should have.

DIAN FOSSEY SPENT the better part of eighteen years among the mountain gorillas of Rwanda. She was to them what Jane Goodall is to the chimpanzees of Tanzania: she devoted her life to them and made us aware of their existence. In 1967 she pitched camp at ten thousand feet in the Virunga Mountains, a chain of mostly extinct volcanoes along the Zaire and Uganda borders. The world's largest population of *Gorilla gorilla beringei*—around 240 individuals, in some twenty groups, each led by a dominant silverback male—lives in the Virungas. It took several years before one of the groups would allow her to sit with them while they chomped celery, groomed each other, played, quarreled, and made love. Dian's habituation of the gorillas was all the more remarkable because she did it without "provisioning"; Goodall had to bribe the chimps with bananas to get their cooperation. After eleven thousand hours in the field, Dian identified the individuals in four groups from their characteristic noseprints and figured out their probable genealogical relationships; she explored little-understood behavior like infanticide and the migration of females among groups. Her scientific work was, according to a colleague, "very factual and detailed. It had the ring of authenticity. She left the theorizing to others." But it was her popular work—a book, *Gorillas in the Mist*; three articles in *National Geographic*; a documentary film about her; and her lectures—that had the greatest impact.

Dian became a feminist icon in America and England—the prototypical gutsy lady doing her thing. In Rwanda she became a legend. The people called her Nyiramacibili, the Woman Who Lives Alone in the Forest. Dian used her prominence to dispel the myth that gorillas are vicious and dangerous—in fact they are among the gentlest of primates—and to bring their plight to the world's attention. During the late seventies an alarming number of mountain gorillas were killed by poachers. One of the gorillas, whom Dian had named Digit, she had a special rapport with; there was no one Digit's age in his group to play with, so he gravitated to her. On December 31, 1977, Digit was found in the forest with his head and hands hacked off. The grisly murder was announced by Walter Cronkite on the "CBS Evening News," and there was a surge of interest in gorilla conservation.

After Digit's death, Dian's war with the poachers became personal. She was increasingly abrasive and explosive, and alienated many people. Early on the morning of December 27, 1985, a few weeks before her fifty-fourth birthday, somebody she had alienated badly, or perhaps a hired assailant, or perhaps just a thief, broke into her cabin and killed her with a machete. There is no shortage of theories about the brutal murder, but it has not been solved, and it may never be. It may remain hidden in the bosom of Africa forever, along with many other mysteries.

THE MODERN WESTERN reverence for wild animals, which gave rise to the wildlife-conservation movement and impelled Dian to dedicate herself to the mountain gorillas, dates from the late nineteenth century. In the beginning of the movement it was still perfectly fine, while setting parks aside and founding flora-and-fauna-protection societies, to bag a trophy or two. The pioneer conservationist Carl Akeley, for instance, thought mountain gorillas were gentle and wonderful, but had no qualms about shooting several for display in the Hall of African Mammals at the American Museum of Natural History. It was Akeley who persuaded King Albert of Belgium to include the Virungas in a national park. In 1926 Akeley returned there to do an in-depth field study of the gorillas, but he died of malaria before he could begin, and was buried in the Kabara meadow, about three hours' walk from where Dian would set up her research station.

It wasn't until the following decade that the first long-term observations of mammals in the wild were made, by the primatologist C. R. Carpenter, who studied howler monkeys on Barro Colorado Island, off Panama. After that there was a lull in overseas field work until the late fifties, when the launching of *Sputnik* made money available in America for scientific work of all kinds, and biologists such as Irven DeVore of Harvard and George Schaller of the University of Wisconsin were able to go to Africa and study baboons and mountain gorillas in their element. More than anyone it was Schaller who, with subsequent studies of tigers, lions, wild sheep and goats, and pandas, popularized the profession of going out and living with the animal of your choice—field biology. His book on the ecology and behavior of mountain gorillas, published in 1963, had a great effect on Dian, who was then already a confirmed animal lover but was working as an occupational therapist in Louisville, Kentucky, still groping her way to her real lifework.

In general, people who are drawn to nature and become animal lovers fall into two groups, which might be described as the Shakespeareans and the Thoreauvians. The Shakespeareans consider man and his works to be part of nature; while loving animals, they have warm, positive feelings toward people, too. The animal love of the Thoreauvians, however, is inversely proportionate to their compassion for their own kind. Often their problems with people, and their sometimes extraordinary empathy with animals, can be traced to a lonely childhood. Most fanatical animal lovers, such as the militant British animal-rights activists who sneak up on fishermen and push them into the river, are Thoreauvians. Another example is Joy Adamson, who did a great deal for lions but was killed by one of her African workers, whom she had abused terribly, in a crime that may closely resemble Dian's murder.

Dian was an only child. Her parents divorced when she was little, and when she was six her mother, Hazel, married a builder named Richard Price. There doesn't seem to have been much love between Dian and her stepfather. Until she was ten, she dined in the kitchen with the housekeeper (the Prices lived in San Francisco and were pretty well off), while her parents ate together in the dining room. As an adult, Dian was estranged from the Prices.

As a child she took lessons at the St. Francis Riding Academy, and she remained horse-crazy through adolescence. She won a letter on the riding team at Lowell High School, where she excelled academically and shunned the cliques that were so important to the other girls. From Lowell she went to the University of California at Davis to study animal husbandry, but after two years there she switched her major to occupational therapy and transferred to San Jose State. In 1955—she was now twenty-three years old and looking for a job—she saw an ad for an occupational therapist at a crippled children's hospital in Louisville and applied, because Kentucky was horse country, she would later say. There she worked with children suffering from polio (this was just before the Salk vaccine) and with inbred mountain children suffering from birth defects; she had a succession of dogs and was "a neat person to be with—generous to a fault, extraordinarily disciplined, with a delightful, self-deprecating sense of humor, tall, slim, perfectly gorgeous," a woman friend recalls.

In 1963, Dian took out a three-year bank loan and went to Africa to see the animals. At Olduvai Gorge in Tanzania she looked up Louis Leakey, the eminent anthropologist who had revolutionized the study of human origins. From Tanzania she went to the Kabara meadow in the Congo, where Schaller had done his research and Akeley was buried. There she met a couple from Kenya, Joan and Alan Root, who were doing a photographic documentary on mountain gorillas. They took her out to see some. "Peeking through the vegetation, we could distinguish an equally curious phalanx of black, leather-countenanced, furry-headed primates peering back at us," she later wrote. She felt a rush of awe, an immediate connection with the huge, magnificent creatures.

After seven weeks in Africa, Dian returned to Louisville and her job. She published articles with her photographs of gorillas and got engaged to a wealthy Southern Rhodesian who was studying at Notre Dame. Three years later Louis Leakey came to town on a lecture tour. One of Leakey's pet projects, after his own work with fossils, was to encourage research on man's closest relatives, the great apes—chimpanzees, orang-utans, gorillas. Leakey had a theory that the best person to go out and study apes was a single woman with no scientific training. Such a person would be unbiased about the behavior she witnessed; unattached, with no responsibilities, she would be willing to work for nothing. A woman would pose less of a threat to the local people (hardly the case with Dian, as it turned out). Women were tougher and more tenacious than men, Leakey believed, and more observant. The truth was, also, that Leakey liked to have women around. He would put them up in a dormitory in the Tigoni Centre for Prehistory and Paleontology in Kenya. There are nearly a hundred Leakey women nobody has ever heard about, who didn't quite make the grade.

The shrewdness of Leakey's theory had been borne out by Jane Goodall's resounding success with chimps, and later Biruté Galdikas would pull through for him with her work on the orangutans of Borneo. But in 1966 he was looking for a "gorilla girl," and after a brief interview with Dian he saw that she had the requisite gumption and offered her the job. Leakey warned her that she would have to have a pre-emptive appendectomy. She swallowed and said no problem. Six weeks later he wrote to say that actually there was no real need for her to have her appendix removed; he had just been testing her determination. But by then it was already out.

Dian's truly admirable efforts on behalf of the gorillas began with her return to Africa at the end of 1966. Leakey set her up with funding, and he retained a close, and more than professional, interest in Dian for the rest of his life. She visited Jane Goodall for a few days to see how she had set up her camp, then proceeded to the Kabara meadow, where she hoped to base her study. But the situation in the Congo was precarious. After six months civil war broke out. Dian was taken off the mountain by rebel Congolese soldiers and held in a place called Rumangabo. She persuaded the soldiers to drive with her into Uganda, leading them to believe that they would be getting her Land-

Rover and some money she had there. When they reached Uganda she managed to have the soldiers arrested. There is a theory that these same soldiers, whom she made such fools of, were her murderers. The merits of this theory are that Zaire, as the Congo is now called, is only a ten-minute walk from her cabin and the frontier is open, and that the way she was killed is more Zaïrois than Rwandan: the Rwandans are a peaceful people who abhor violence. If a Rwandan wanted to kill someone he would use poison. The problem with the theory—a big one—is why would the soldiers have waited eighteen years?

IN THE FALL of 1967, Dian set up a new study site on the Rwanda side of the Virungas. For the first few years she had the help of a Belgian woman who lived there, Alyette DeMunck. Alyette had just lost her son and nephew, to whom she had given a trip to Africa as a graduation present from their university in Belgium. The two young men had driven down from Kampala to see her and had taken a wrong turn into the Congo, where they were arrested and killed by soldiers who thought they were mercenaries. Alyette helped Dian choose the saddle between Mounts Karisimbi and Visoke as her new base, which Dian, combining the two names, called Karisoke, and she negotiated with the local people who built the cabins. Dian was hopeless at languages.

In 1968 the National Geographic Society, which was sponsoring Dian, sent a photographer named Bob Campbell to film her at work. Bob was from Kenya—tall, quiet, kind, a devoted conservationist and a fine photographer who has accompanied the Duke of Edinburgh on safari. A "tenderness" developed between them, as one of Dian's friends delicately phrased it, since Bob was married. He spent several months at a time on the mountain with her until 1972. "Bob was perfect for her—

a calming influence," the friend recalled. His movie is a poignant record of her early years at Karisoke. The footage is not exactly *cinéma vérité*; there is a slight flush of self-consciousness on Dian's face as she pretends to be absorbed in note-taking or walks before a breathtaking bit of scenery. She was always a little self-conscious about her six-foot height, and complained to friends that she wished she were more "stacked," but she is definitely a good-looking woman, willowy, with an Irish twinkle, and she looks very happy. Her voice is worldly, self-possessed, laid-back California. It has none of the innocence of some naturalists'. In one sequence Dian is sitting with a gorilla. The gorilla takes Dian's notebook, looks at it carefully, and politely passes it back, then does the same with her pencil—such a familiar, friendly interaction that you almost forget the gorilla isn't human. A few minutes later Dian and her student, Kelly Stewart, are watching gorillas together. Kelly looks just like her dad, the actor Jimmy Stewart. What an idyllic life, one thinks as Dian romps in her high rubber boots among *Hagenia* trees dripping with strands of lichen, looking here and there for gorillas. Everything at Karisoke—the cluster of tin-sided shacks high in the montane forest, Dian's home, which she created from nothing—seems harmonious.

In fact, Dian "was under enormous pressures that few people knew about," according to Bob Campbell, whom I reached by telephone. He now lives outside Nairobi, not far from where Karen Blixen had her coffee plantation. "She had to construct the camp and keep it going. It was very hard to get supplies, and her funds were meager. There were a couple of students who didn't work out—who came looking for a fabulous life in the bush and couldn't take the harsh conditions. Nothing is easy up there. She had to help Alyette through her tragedy, and she herself had suffered severely during the Congo rebellion, when she was held by the soldiers at Rumangabo."

How? I asked. "She was always reluctant to describe it," Bob said. Was she tortured? I asked. "No," Bob said. "She was not harmed physically." Was she sexually molested? "Yes," he said, "and this experience set her attitudes toward the local people."

THE MAIN EXTERNAL PROBLEM for both Dian and Bob at that time was that the gorillas were wild and unapproachable and afraid of humans. The only people they had had contact with were the Batutsi cattle herders and the "poachers." The Batutsi are the famous Watusi—tall, lanky Hamitic warrior-pastoralists who came down from the north some four hundred years ago and subjugated the Bahutu—short, stocky Bantu agriculturists who had come from the south even earlier. When Rwanda won independence from Belgium in 1962, the Bahutu rose up and slaughtered their former masters. Thousands of Batutsi fled into the forests of the Parc des Volcans, driving with them tens of thousands of head of lyre-horned Ankole cattle. No one minded that these people and their stock were in the park, disturbing the gorillas, until Dian came along.

Most of the poachers in the forest are Batwa Pygmies—Rwanda's third, and original, ethnic group. The Batwa have been hunter-gatherers since time immemorial. They are poachers only by recent legislative fiat. Like their cousins, the Bambuti and the Efe Pygmies in the Ituri Forest of Zaire, they are a fun-loving people, mischievous, ready to dance at the drop of a hat. Incredibly alert in the forest, they have as little as possible to do with farming, which they consider dull, hot, demeaning work. The main quarry of the Batwa are forest antelope—bushbucks and black-fronted duikers—for which they lay snares. An antelope steps into one and, whoosh, he is hoisted into the air.

Occasionally one of Dian's gorillas would get a hand or a foot caught in a Batwa snare. It would usually struggle free, but its wrist or ankle would be a bloody mess, gangrene would set in, and often it would end up dying a month or two later. Understandably, when this happened Dian would be very upset. She considered the Batwa, and the handful of Bahutu who live among them and organize them and make use of their superior hunting abilities, the main threat to the gorillas, and as time went on she devoted increasing energy to cutting their snares, destroying their traps, raiding their villages, terrorizing and punishing them.

How much Dian's war on the local cattle herders and hunters was motivated by concern for the gorillas, and how much it served as an outlet for her Thoreauvian antipathy to people, especially to Africans, after what had happened at Rumangabo, is hard to say. There are many different views of Dian. People either loved her or loathed her. In general, the Dian lovers are women who knew her in the States, socially, or through her warm, funny, generous-spirited letters, while the Dian haters are fellow scientists who were up on the mountain with her. The lovers describe the haters as "aggressive Young Turks who were in competition with her," while the haters describe the lovers' perception of her as "rose-tinted." Very few people were aware of what happened at Rumangabo. The experience must have burned into her being, as the torture and sodomy T. E. Lawrence suffered from Turks did into his.

Bob Campbell remains one of her staunch defenders. "She was caught up in circumstances beyond her control, disasters that upset her mind in the early stages and soured her later years. Others would have quit. She was never physically strong, but she had guts and will power and an urgent desire to study the gorillas, and that was what kept her up there." I asked him how close their relationship had been. "Close enough that she didn't want me to leave," he said. "She came to rely on me for many things that weren't part of my assignment— running the staff, dealing with the students. After six months we reached an agreement that we were both up there to work for the gorillas, but even so, I left before my assignment was completed." Friends remember that Dian was devastated by Bob's departure. The part of her that yearned for a mate and children was shattered.

THE PRIMATOLOGICAL COMMUNITY, which had mixed feelings about Dian, is a small, intense one. It isn't easy for primatologists to get funded, and university positions and opportunities to work in the field are limited. This forces them into competition with one another. In order to get a Ph.D. the primatologist must go out into the field for a year or two, alone or with several colleagues, and collect data. This is the critical phase of his or her career, because a scientist who doesn't have data doesn't have anything. It is also the most stressful phase. You have to adapt to primitive living conditions, an alien environment and culture, and isolation. The field work itself is a constant worry. Maybe your line of reasoning will turn out to be all wrong and you'll have to come up with a new hypothesis and collect entirely different data. Maybe somebody will come up with a better approach to your problem and solve it before you do. Maybe— this is a huge worry—somebody will rip off your data. Or maybe your data will be lost or destroyed. (This happened to Kelly Stewart, who was collecting data at Karisoke for a Ph.D. from Cambridge. One night she hung her wet clothes too close to the wood stove in her cabin, and while she was having dinner at Dian's cabin, eighteen months' worth of field notes went up in smoke.) And during all this time you get little or no feedback. The animals certainly aren't going to tell you if you're on the right track.* "It's very lonely up there," the primatologist Ann Pierce, who spent fourteen months at Karisoke tracking lesser-known groups, told me. "You keep waiting for Tarzan to swing down from the trees. You fantasize and keep going and a lot of the time you feel like you're the luckiest person in the whole world."

Dian was not academically qualified to study gorillas, and that always bothered her. She felt in the shadow of Schaller, who in eighteen months had picked up probably eighty to ninety percent of what there is to learn about mountain gorillas, at least at our present level of understanding. So in 1973 she went back to college. If she was going to get continued support, she was going to have to get a degree. She enrolled in the sub-department of animal behaviour at Darwin College, Cambridge, under Robert Hinde, Jane Goodall's supervisor, and fell in with some brilliant young primatologists. For the next few years she went back and forth between Cambridge and Africa.

There had been a tremendous surge of environmental awareness in the West while Dian was on the mountain. *Ecology*, an abstruse scientific term, had become a household word. The baby boomers were getting Ph.D.s in record numbers from newly created or expanded natural science departments. A new breed of biologist was arriving to do field work in the African bush, bringing new political attitudes, an openness to the local people,

---

*Some people who are familiar with the inner workings of the primatological community have been struck by similarities between primate behavior and that of the primatologists themselves. When one's career is devoted to the study of things like territoriality, dominance, access to resources and fertile females, and genetic self-interest, some of it is bound to rub off. Sarah Hrdy, one of a number of scientists (most of them women) who have reexamined the social behavior of baboons and concluded that the females play a far more important role than the early work of Irven DeVore gave them credit for, has noticed these similarities. "DeVore's paradigm, which has a central male hierarchy with the males competing among themselves and making alliances to stay in power, i.e., to control access to the fertile females, was a more accurate portrayal of what goes on in American graduate schools, with the big man bringing up his protégés and sleeping with impressionable undergraduates, than of anything that goes on in baboon society," Hrdy told me recently.

a willingness to learn their language, to include their needs and point of view in conservation strategies. The only way you can save animals in the Third World, these new-wave biologists realized, is to make the animals worth more to the local people alive than dead, to give them a stake in their survival.

Dian was intimidated by the young scientists who came to Karisoke to study with her. She felt that they were more interested in their graphs of gorilla reproductive success than in the gorillas themselves. They weren't willing to interrupt their observation schedules to go and cut snares. She believed that the local people were lazy, corrupt, and incompetent, and that there was no point in trying to work with them. Her first priority was to stop the poaching. The young scientists felt her war with the poachers was nasty and inappropriate, and they didn't want to be associated with it.

IN 1977 Digit was murdered and mutilated, and Dian "came to live within an insulated part of myself," as she wrote in her book. She was increasingly reclusive and morose and peculiar, retreating even from the gorillas. During one eighteen-month period in the late seventies she went out to the gorillas only six times, when important visitors—a film crew, the American ambassador and his wife, big contributors to gorilla conservation—came up. On these occasions she pulled herself together and was charming, but by this time she was a sick and increasingly bitter woman. She had emphysema, for which two packs a day of Impala *filtrée*, the strong local cigarettes, were doing no good. She began to drink. Communications with other researchers in the camp took place mainly through notes.

Dian's consuming interest was in punishing the poachers. Once she put a noose around a captured Pygmy, threw the rope over a rafter, and threatened to hoist him if he didn't start talking. Horrible rumors began circulating among the Belgian doctors in

Kigali: that she had injected one poacher with gorilla dung to give him septicemia; that she had hired a sorcerer to poison another particularly incorrigible one.

Dian's treatment of the poachers didn't really bother the Rwandan authorities, since the park guards were just as brutal once she turned the poachers over to them. What the Rwandans resented was her open contempt for them. Dian was convinced that they were all corrupt. She publicly accused the *conservateur* of the park of being behind the attempted abduction of one young gorilla, at a time when the park officials were finally beginning to take their job seriously. There was a big row between Dian and the Rwandan Organization for Tourism and National Parks, the agency that controls foreign visitors to the country's national parks, over David Attenborough, who had asked Dian if he could shoot a gorilla sequence for his "Life on Earth" series. Dian said fine. Until then she had been allowed to invite up anybody she wanted to. Attenborough went up with a crew, but when he came down he was harassed for not having a permit from ORTPN, which wanted to assert its control over park visitors. Dian was furious. So bad were the relations between her and the director of tourism, Laurent Habiyaremye, that some Rwandans and European expatriates believe it was he who had her killed. According to this theory, Habiyaremye wanted to get rid of Dian so ORTPN could take over Karisoke and turn it into a tourist facility, convert the groups of gorillas used for research into tourist groups, and make that much more money. A spokesman for ORTPN told me that if they had wanted to take over Karisoke they wouldn't have had to kill her; they could have just ordered her to leave. He said they wanted Karisoke to remain a research center that would one day be run by Rwandans.

THE MOUNTAIN GORILLA proved to be as good a fund-raising animal as the panda or the whale. As money began to pour in,

Dian agreed for it to be channeled through the African Wildlife Foundation, which was already set up to process donations. But there was a big blowup over how the money should be used. Dian wanted it with no strings attached, to beef up her anti-poaching patrols, to implement what she called "active conservation." Her refusal to cooperate with the Rwandans and the things she was doing to the poachers were unacceptable to the AWF, so Dian ended up pulling out with her Digit Fund, and accusing the AWF of stealing her money. The AWF joined with other conservation groups to fund the Mountain Gorilla Project, which takes a three-pronged approach to saving the gorillas: set up tourism as a way of providing Rwanda with income from the animals and a reason for keeping them alive; train and increase the number of park guards; and educate the local people about the value of the gorillas and their habitat. In 1978 two young Americans, Bill Weber and Amy Vedder, came out to help set up the project while working on respective Ph.D.s on the socioeconomic aspects of conservation and on the feeding ecology of the mountain gorilla. Bill and Amy were a couple (Dian had particular trouble dealing with couples), and an extremely dynamic one. Amy was everything Dian was not: a highly trained zoologist who spoke French and got on well with Africans, a wife and mother to boot. So jealousy was probably a factor in the bad blood that developed between them. But it was also that Dian couldn't stomach the idea of tourists, whom she called "idle rubberneckers," being marched up to see the gorillas. She thought the tourism was going to be handled the way it is in Zaire, where twenty or thirty tourists at a shot are taken up by a dozen Pygmies who cut a wide swath in the vegetation right up to the gorillas and taunt them into beating their chests and screaming and charging. In 1980 she fired several shots over the heads of a party of Dutch tourists who had hiked up to Karisoke uninvited.

It became increasingly clear to friends and foes alike that Dian's presence at Karisoke had become counterproductive and possibly even dangerous to herself. Bill Weber drafted a letter to the National Geographic Society, Dian's main backer, describing how badly run Karisoke was and speculating on a link between her persecution of the poachers and the fact that the only gorillas who were being killed were the ones in her study groups. This letter found its way into the hands of a friend of Dian's at the American embassy, who showed it to Dian. She was already convinced that there was a conspiracy to get rid of her. Now she had evidence. She took to sneaking up on the researchers' cabins at night and listening to their conversations, to opening and reading their mail.

WEBER THREATENED to send his critical letter if the American ambassador, Frank Crigler, didn't get her out of the country, and Crigler spent "an enormous amount of government time," as he told me, on what was a private-sector problem—trying to find an academic institution where she could go and write her book, which she was under increasing pressure to produce. Harvard and other institutions were approached, but none were interested. Finally Cornell offered her a visiting associate professorship, and in 1980 she left for Ithaca, where she stayed three years before returning to Karisoke.

While Dian was in Ithaca, Sandy Harcourt, one of the new-wave zoologists, a bright, handsome, reserved, ambitious young Englishman, took over as director of Karisoke. He is one of the leading experts on *Gorilla gorilla beringei*. Sandy had spent several years on the mountain with Dian in the mid-seventies. They started out friends, but then Kelly Stewart, of whom Dian was very fond, began living with Sandy. Dian's antipathy toward couples surfaced, and she turned on them.

The Harcourts (Sandy and Kelly got married in 1977) live outside Cambridge, but I reached them in Beverly Hills, where they were visiting Kelly's parents for a few days, on their way to a primate center in Japan. Sandy didn't want to talk about Dian. A number of primatologists didn't want to talk about Dian, because they felt that the negative things they would have to say would do nobody any good, especially the gorillas, with whom she is identified. Richard Wrangham, who knew Dian at Cambridge and has since become one of the most respected people in the field, didn't want to criticize her because he felt that it is "the ones like her, with fires in their bellies, who make the real contributions, not the ones who take courses until they're thirty-five, go out into the field for six months, and teach at Podunk U. for the rest of their lives."

But Kelly wanted to talk about Dian. "The first time I saw gorillas was in the summer of 1972, in Zaire," she began. "I had graduated from Stanford with a degree in anthropology and I was on a tourist trip and I went up to see the eastern-lowland gorillas near Bukavu. I was so amazed, I knew I wanted to work with them. So I wrote Dian—I'd read her *National Geographic* article—and asked if she needed anybody, a gofer, a research assistant, anything. After she got the letter, she met me at Stanford to check me out. At the first meeting and for a long time afterward I idolized her, because of the minigod syndrome of the academic big guys: you feel this incredible admiration, you want to be like them. That's how a lot of the students thought of her, until they got to Karisoke.

"When I got there in 1974 she was engaged to a French doctor in Ruhengeri [a good-size town below the mountain], but that didn't work out. She broke up with him near the end of 1975. The problem was that she wasn't willing to leave Karisoke, and he didn't want to live up there. Her trouble with relationships was that she could never give herself completely; she always pulled back because she wanted to keep her independence. She was always lonely and always talked about wanting to marry and have a family, but it was her fault that she never did. Her trouble with relationships was that she wanted them and she didn't. Biruté Galdikas [the third "Leakey lady"] married a Dayak head man, but Dian did not consider that strategy.

"She had a perfectly colonial attitude toward the Africans. On Christmas she'd give the most extravagant presents to them; other times she'd humiliate them, spit on the ground in front of them—once I even saw her spit *on* one of the workers—break into their cabin and accuse them of stealing and dock their pay. Two researchers left Karisoke because of the way she treated the Africans. 'My people,' she called them, like Blixen. They were loyal to her, but they had to stay because there are few paid jobs in the area and there is a certain cachet to being a tracker. The men never knew when she was going to start yelling at them. That was how she treated the rest of us, too. One minute she'd pile on praise to an embarrassing extent, the next day she'd berate you. When she left camp it was like a cloud had risen, and it got worse over the years."

Soon after her funeral, five of Dian's trackers—Bahutu she had hired from the villages below—were arrested and placed in the Ruhengeri prison, where they were held for months without charges. The *panga*, the heavy-bladed local machete that was used to kill her and was found under her bed, was from the camp. Prints were unobtainable because it had been passed from hand to hand at the scene of the crime.

According to one theory, the trackers were taken into custody because of a cultural misunderstanding. At Dian's funeral, Amy Vedder went up to Nemeye, one of the trackers, and hugged him. This was a very American thing to do at a funeral, but not a Rwandan one at all. Rwandans shake hands vigorously upon meeting, they don't hug. The police, who were at the funeral looking for anything out of the ordinary and knew that there was bad blood between Dian and Amy, saw her hug Nemeye and assumed the two of them were in cahoots, so Nemeye and the four others were taken in. But, Ann Pierce told me, "It's inconceivable any of the men could have killed her. They're like Sherpas. They get tickled and look sheepish when you get angry at them." Kelly Stewart agreed. "The guys in jail are really good guys," she told me. "It's not possible any of them could have done it." Many other Karisoke veterans agree with her. Subscribers to the tracker theory offer two motives: money and revenge for humiliation. African men, they argue, find it very hard to be dressed down by a woman.

Other theories focus on the Bahutu poachers who live with the Batwa. They certainly had reason to want her out of the picture. Dian had at least one mortal enemy, the poacher Munyarukiko. Munyarukiko was a real killer, and he hated Dian. She had broken into his house and destroyed his possessions and kidnapped his boy (who was well treated, and told Dian a lot about the poaching). He had been involved in the death of Digit and may have been the one who shot Uncle Bert, the dominant silverback male in Digit's group, in an act many believe was a vendetta against Dian. Munyarukiko could have reasoned that the sweetest revenge he could inflict on her was to kill her gorillas one by one, before he got her. But Munyarukiko died in 1978, or so Dian heard from local informants. According to one story, he ran away with a woman to Uganda and the woman's people tracked them there and killed him. But is Munyarukiko really dead?

In May of that year another notorious poacher, Sebahutu, was caught, but he was in jail in December, so that rules him out, at least as the actual murderer. Then, on November 14, Hatageka, whom Dian described as "one of the last of the old-timers," was caught skinning a bushbuck fifty yards from the park boundary. Hatageka was brought to Dian. In a letter to Ian Redmond, who went to Karisoke in 1976 to study the parasites in the gorillas' dung and in his two years there became increasingly involved in antipoaching work, she wrote, "I *gently* examined his clothing and sewn in his sleeve was a small pouch of *sumu* [poison in Swahili], containing bits of vegetation and skin, all looking like vacuum cleaner debris." Dian took the bits and put them on her mantelpiece. While she was in her bedroom getting a reward for the guards for bringing Hatageka in, he lunged for the pieces. The guards subdued him and Dian took them back. Then Hatageka was led away. "I still have them," Dian wrote. "Nasty lady. It was like taking a nipple from a baby. He just deflated after I took them." Redmond's theory, which has received a lot of attention in the American press, is that Hatageka sent someone to break into the cabin and get back his *sumu*. (Incarceration in Africa is a lot more relaxed than it is in the West. Food, women, dope, a trip to the market are only a question of money. There is ample opportunity to plot revenge with your brothers, to arrange with someone on the outside to get the person who put you there.) Dian awakened. The burglar panicked, grabbed a handy machete, and killed her. When Ian was collecting her personal effects to send to her parents several weeks after the murder, he found in a drawer a Ziploc bag containing what looked like the *sumu*. He also found the letter to him, dated November 24 but never sent, describing the capture of Hatageka.

It is perfectly possible that a Bahutu, particularly one in as dangerous a profession as poaching, might carry a protective talisman, although a more correct word for it would be *impigi*, not *sumu*. "The talisman could be a little packet of herbs, the tooth of an animal, a piece of antelope horn—no telling what," the anthropologist Chris Taylor, who studies traditional Bahutu medicine, told me. "Children are thought to be particularly vulnerable to witchcraft, and are often given a leather thong to wear around the waist to ward it off."

Ian Redmond, whom I reached at his home in Bristol, England, said that he never saw a talisman on any of the dozen poachers with whom he had direct contact. "But this isn't something they're going to show you," he added. "Only after my return to England did Dian become aware that if you got the poacher's talisman that really weakens him and gives you a psychological advantage."

It is also possible that a Bahutu might kill to get his talisman back. He would be afraid that whoever had it could use it to work a spell against him and do him great harm. The belief that illness is caused by the magic of an enemy, or by actual poison, is widespread in black Africa. The cure is to hire a healer to identify the enemy and to work a counterspell. Moreover, if someone had suffered a dreadful family misfortune and had attributed it to Dian (who to scare the poachers cultivated the image of a witch), that could have been the end of her. But would avengers have come unarmed? That's a problem with this theory.

Dian's treatment of the poachers, as Kelly described it, was merciless. "She would torture them. She would whip their balls with stinging nettles, spit on them, kick them, put on masks and curse them, stuff sleeping pills down their throats. She said she hated doing it, and respected the poachers for being able to live in the forest, but she got into it and liked to do it and felt guilty that she did. She hated them so much. She reduced them to quivering, quaking packages of fear, little guys in rags rolling on the ground and foaming at the mouth."

Some of Dian's friends condone her methods with the poachers. Ian said he never actually saw Dian lay a hand on anyone. "A lot of her alleged mistreatment was not stopping the guards." He had heard stories about Dian whipping the Pygmies' balls with stinging nettles, "and I know how that is going to sound to the tender-skinned European reader sitting in his armchair, but don't forget that the Pygmies run through stinging nettles every week," he argued. Ian himself recently advocated equipping the antipoaching patrols with submachine guns. He also defended Dian's treatment of the camp staff. "If you're working with Africans and want them to perform up to European standards, you have to blow up at them, because they try to get away with doing as little as possible." He is the only person besides Bob Campbell and Alyette DeMunck who was with Dian on the mountain for any length of time and remained her friend. "Dian as an individual was in many ways like the gorillas," he told another journalist, "in that if you are easily put off by bluff charges, screaming and shouting, then you probably think that the gorillas are monsters. But if you are prepared to sidestep the bluff charges and temper and shouting and get to know the person within . . . then you'll find that Dian, like the gorilla, was a gentle, loving person."

Kelly Stewart wasn't so magnanimous. "I think by the end she was doing more harm than good," she told me. "Dian went out to the gorillas because she loved them and she loved the bush and being on her own, but she ended up with more than she bargained for. [She wasn't planning on having to organize and work with and fight with people.] She was no good as a scientific mentor, but she couldn't hand over control. She couldn't take the back seat. Her alternative—to leave and die somewhere an invalid—was never something she would have considered. She always fantasized about a final confrontation. She viewed herself as a warrior fighting this enemy who was out to get her. It was a perfect ending. She got what she wanted. It was exactly how she would have ended the script. It must have been painful, but it didn't last long. The first whack killed her. It was such a clean whack I understand there was hardly any blood."

• • •

THE BANYARWANDA IN Kigali are unaware of what Nyiramacibili was like on the mountain or that she called them "woggiepoos." To them she is a national hero. "She was a good
woman," a man standing in the moonlight in front of the Mille
Collines tells me. "Did you know her?" I ask. "Several times.
It was she who showed us the gorillas." And the Batutsi woman
who rents me a jeep: "She was *très courageuse*. A courageous
woman like that they should have left alone. They should have
put up a statue to her. She lived alone and consecrated her life
to the gorillas. That is very rare."

I hired a driver, a young man named Abdallah Issa, who
had been Dian's taximan whenever she was in Kigali. "She was
très, très gentille, monsieur," he told us. "*Je regrette encore*. She
gave me this *cowboy* [the jeans he was wearing] from America.
For this I am against the people who killed her."

It is a two-hour drive to Ruhengeri, where the police station
is. Weaving through "the land of a thousand hills," the road is
a busy river, flowing with blue-uniformed schoolgirls, women
balancing crocks of banana beer on their heads, firewood, bundles of wash. Out in the countryside, not a tree is left of the
original forest. Abdallah drives slowly through a crowd gathered
around a man on a bicycle who has just been struck dead by a
minibus. The public transport stops for no one. I flick a cigarette
to the side of the road. A boy picks it up and runs along with
us, smoking it with the hot tip in his mouth. Another boy calls
shamelessly, "Give me money. I have nothing to eat." Ruhengeri
is a beautiful town. The air is thin and spiced and full of birds.

I get nowhere with Mathias Bushishi, the public prosecutor
in charge of the investigation, who says, "As soon as the in-
vestigations are concluded, we will certainly publish the *dé-
nouement*. As you say, Nyiramacibili is very important to us and

to America, and we can hardly overlook the matter or keep it secret, but"—he gives an apologetic shrug—"my hands are tied." What happens in general when someone is murdered? I ask. How do you find out who did it? "In general," Bushishi explains, "when a murder is unsolved, one continues to search, over a period known as *la préscription de l'infraction* [which is like our statute of limitations]. We try to break the conspiracy of silence. We listen to people in bars, talking in the market, at private *réunions*. We bring people in for questioning. Many people may know, but they aren't talking. But time is on our side. Sooner or later somebody will say something he will regret. *La préscription de l'infraction* lasts ten years. But in this case we are in a hurry."

The Rwandan theory, which I heard from a man who said he had it from "someone close to the investigation," is this: Dian was happy with everybody except the Americans who worked with her. She made more money than they did. One day two Zaïrois were hired by two American ex-students to get rid of her. The Zaïrois hired the men who worked in the camp to go through her window late one night and kill her. According to my source, two of the workers were taken in for questioning, and after many beatings they said there were three others. The "evidence" for this theory is: "American" hair was found near the body. A thousand dollars in cash was left in the cabin. No Rwandan would have passed it up. Finally, Rwandans simply don't kill *bazungu*. The last time was something like thirty years ago, when a European woman was murdered by a Rwandan she had sacked for stealing. No, this had to be the work of foreigners. There seemed to be a political dimension to this theory as well, just as the Rwandan stance on AIDS is that the *bazungu* brought it into the country. (In fact the virus is thought by many Western scientists to be endemic to Central Africa, and Rwanda is one of the countries where the AIDS epidemic is most severe.)

But why would Dian's students have wanted to kill her? I asked my source. To get her documents, he explained. What "documents"? Her notes. But of what value are they to anybody? She wrote a book and made a lot of money, and was spending most of her time in the cabin writing another book. Whoever got his hands on the notes could make a lot of money himself. A few days later I heard from an expatriate American another explanation of why Rwandans think Dian's notes are worth a lot of money: the Rwandans watch all these Americans going into the forest, which is crazy in the first place, and figure there must be a gold mine up there. They see the Americans taking notes all the time, so obviously the gold mine must be in the notes.

DIAN'S OLDEST AND dearest friend in Rwanda, Rosamond Carr, has a flower farm in the hills above Lake Kivu, an hour from Ruhengeri. Her cottage is nestled in a formal English garden which was in spectacular bloom the day I visited. This was another Africa, the Africa of Blixen, of devoted houseboys, a gracious, bygone Africa where roles were well defined and the meaning of life was clear. Mrs. Carr, a glamorous, gray-haired woman of about seventy, came to the door and—showing me into her cozy living room, with a fireplace, rugs, pillows, a pet gray parrot on a stand, lots of books, old *New Yorkers* on the table—called into the kitchen for her cook to bring tea. She apologized for being temporarily understaffed. Her houseboy had taken the day off to look after his sick daughter. "She may have grippe," Mrs. Carr explained. "He thinks she was poisoned by an enemy, and is paying a Rwandan woman a month's salary to treat her.

"Dian was the dearest, sweetest person," she told me. "Oh God, she was just marvelous to her friends. Knowing I have foot problems, she once brought me twenty-four dollars' worth of Dr. Scholl's foot pads. These scientists—they're so jealous of each other, so unkind. Some of them were the pits, real weirdos. One was gay. The other was on drugs. One I practically threw out of my house."

Mrs. Carr grew up in New Jersey, obviously on the right side of the tracks, married a British coffee grower, and came to Africa in 1949. "I knew Dian from the beginning, right after she was chased out of the Congo," she went on. "I introduced her to Alyette DeMunck. My impression at first was that this was a girl who is so dedicated to one idea that she is very eccentric. She had no interest in Africans, only in animals. She and I were completely different in that respect. My falling in love with Africa was with the people. Every Sunday I have dancing for them in my garden. She wanted to get rid of the Africans on the mountain. We had problems because of this. I had great sympathy for the Watusi cattlemen."

Mrs. Carr told me how Alexi, Dian's Rhodesian fiancé from Notre Dame, came to rescue her after her troubles in the Congo and take her home but she refused to go, and about her affair with Bob Campbell, and said that many suitors—young diplomats, well-born Europeans on safari—hoofed it up the mountain after that. "But she was elusive. We all admit she wasn't easy to get on with. When she was disgusted she wasn't as forgiving as she might have been. But the biggest lie is that she was a heavy drinker. She drank less than anybody I know. She visited me a hundred times and never took more than one drink, Scotch and water, before lunch. In her last years she became sweeter. I was her only real friend, and she poured her heart out to me in her letters. She wrote every ten days. Last August I burned a stack of them; I had no idea she was going to be killed. In her last letter she said, Oh, Roz, I need a friend so much. So many people are against me."

• • •

DESPITE DIAN'S OPPOSITION to it, the Mountain Gorilla Project has been a great success. Since 1979 gorilla tourists have increased the Parc des Volcans' receipts by two thousand percent, and the number of guards, guides, and administrators has doubled. Local appreciation of the gorillas and the forest, which is needed not just for the gorillas but to prevent erosion and drought, has grown dramatically. A recent popular Rwandan song goes, "Where can the gorillas go? They are part of our country. They have no other home." In 1979 thirty gorilla skulls were seized, and a prominent European trafficker in gorilla parts was expelled from the country. There hasn't been a known poaching incident involving a gorilla in three years.

Bill Weber, who worked on the project until recently, is not one of Dian's fans. "I only knew the person I had to deal with for eight years," he told me as we sat on the porch of the comfortable colonial villa in Ruhengeri where he lives with Amy Vedder and their children, "and this was a sad person. She was riding on some kind of dedication she had once had. Why did she hardly ever go out to the gorillas if they were her life-motivating force? She criticized others of 'me-itis,' yet she kept threatening to burn the station down and all the long-term records. She was willing to take down everything with her—Karisoke, the gorillas. When I did a census that indicated the gorilla population was growing quite nicely, she tried to cut off my funding; she wanted them to be dying.

"Dian could have had all the accolades in the world for what she did during the first six years. It would have been natural for others to build on her work, but she didn't have the self-confidence or the character for that to happen. So many people came over here inspired by Dian Fossey, prepared to give her the benefit of the doubt. No one wanted to fight her. No one wanted to take over the place. She invented so many plots and enemies. She kept talking about how nobody could take it up there, how they all got 'bushy,' but in the end she was the only one who went bonkers. She didn't get killed because she was saving the gorillas. She got killed because she was behaving like Dian Fossey."

When Dian returned to Rwanda in 1983 she was *"une femme épuisée,"* a worn-out woman, a man with ORTPN told me. She said, not jokingly, that she had come home to die. Three years in America had been a nice break, but there was no place for her there. To Westerners who have been away from the West, the hardest part is coming back. The culture seems tame, self-centered, materialistic, way out of perspective. And what could she have done in the States? She wasn't a success as a teacher or a lecturer. Audiences found her aloof and intimidating. She kept her eyes to the ceiling and once snarled at someone who had interrupted her, "Shut your mouth, child, or I'll shut it for you."

"This time her disposition was excellent," Alain Monfort, a Belgian who had been acting *conservateur* of the Parc des Volcans during Dian's most impossible period, recalled. "Let's forget everything. Start at zero," she told Monfort. The porters carried her up to Karisoke on a stretcher.

THE PATH TO Karisoke is steep and slippery. At every other step I sank into six inches of mud. Twice a gigantic earthworm—sixteen inches long and three-quarters of an inch in diameter—lay in the path. The porters and I rose through the bamboo and nettle zones, and after two hours we reached the saddle between Karisimbi and Visoke. The path leveled out and led through parklike *Hagenia* woodland. Dazzling little birds with names like scarlet-tufted malachite sunbird darted among lichen-bearded branches and drank nectar from showy yellow *Hypericum* flowers. It seemed like a fairyland, except that it was booby-trapped with poachers' snares and full of mean-tempered buffalo—Sandy Harcourt had been almost gored to death by one—and the conditions for field work, what with the altitude, the dampness, the vertical terrain, the mud, the nettles, and the isolation, were very daunting. When I thought of Dian up here for the better part of two decades, replaying over and over what had happened to her at Rumangabo, and all the other abuses and heartbreaks she had suffered, with one after another of the animals she had come to know and love deeply being killed and horribly mutilated, I could see how she might have become a little erratic.

The cabin where I stayed was cozy, with two beds, a writing table, and a wood stove in which my houseboy fired up some deadwood. Then he took my wet, muddy clothes and boots off to be cleaned and came back with a basin of hot water. This is the one luxury at Karisoke—servants. As I sponged off I could see huge white-naped ravens strutting around outside, and reddish, high-haunched, deerlike duikers walking delicately among the trees.

Fifty yards uphill from my cabin was Dian's, still locked and guarded. Even David Watts was unable to get in. It was the largest cabin, at the far end of the camp, with three fireplaces. For a shack it is quite palatial. Fifty yards in the other direction was Wayne McGuire's cabin. Wayne is another American primatologist. He discovered Dian's body and had been holding the fort until David's arrival. I went down to meet him that evening, after he got back from the gorillas. Thirty-four, bearded, with glasses, he seemed a little apprehensive and freaked out, but considering what he had been through, he was holding up remarkably well. Wayne grew up in a lower-middle-class family in Hoboken. There was no money for college. He put himself through the University of Oklahoma, and now, two degrees later, he was collecting data for a dissertation on "The Effects of Male Parental Care on Immature Survival." After sending her his proposal twice and waiting two years, he had been chosen by Dian over dozens of applicants. He and a girlfriend, also a primatologist, were supposed to have come out together, but at the last moment they had broken up. For nine months he had been up here alone, except for Dian during the first five; shifts of camp staff, park guards, and Digit Fund antipoaching patrols, which he'd been having to oversee since her death, although he could barely communicate with them; the gorillas, of course; and a procession of reporters from *The New York Times*, the Washington *Post*, *People*, *Life*, even a crew from the "Today" show, who had slogged up the mountain, asked lots of questions, taken pictures, then headed back down a few hours later. *People*, he told me, had blown out of proportion something he had said, about how Dian had kept a lock of his hair and had used it to control him. True, he had found in Dian's cabin an envelope with the word *Wayne* on it in her writing, and the envelope contained hair that could have been his; but he had no evidence that she was trying to control him. For the first month after the murder, he had slept with a gun. Now he was pretty sure nothing was going to happen. He had fifteen more months of data collecting to do, and, murder or no, he was going to hang in here. "But even a lousy relationship would be better than this," he complained.

Most of the time, he and Dian had gotten along fine. Once or twice a month she would invite him to her cabin to dinner. Occasionally she would explode at him for no reason, but he learned to use "the Gandhi strategy," to let it in one ear and out the other. "Dian was very lonely and vulnerable," he said. "It wasn't that she was a racist, she just disliked human beings. She'd turn her back on people but secretly want to be with them.

Compared to people, the gorillas are so attractive, so accepting, so easy. You can project a whole lot on them."

At Christmas, as a joke, Dian gave Wayne a package of condoms from Ziz, a prolific silverback with eleven mates and twenty-four gorillas in his group. Then, two mornings afterward, at 6:30, the men awaken him and say they can't find Nyiramacibili, which is a delicate way of saying something terrible has happened. He pulls on his long johns and goes up with them to her cabin. The tin sheet under her bedroom window has been snipped out. The living room has been torn apart. The place has been ransacked. They all just stand there in shock. Finally Wayne makes his way into the bedroom, moving away boxes and overturned furniture that block the entrance. Dian is lying on the floor with her head and a shoulder slumped on the bed. At first Wayne thinks she has had a heart attack, but as he draws near to give her artificial respiration he notices a little blood on the sheet under her head, and he sees that she has been whacked clean across the face—he can see into her skull—and also smacked on the back of her head with a blunt instrument. "It looked as if she got hit on the back of the head, rolled out of bed, then got hit across the face," he told me. "It was definitely a setup, a professional hit—fast, quiet, and effective. Someone knew what he was doing." David Watts feels the same way: the murder was a premeditated, long-simmering act related to her personal war with the poachers. Somebody had staked the place out and found that she often drank herself to sleep. The reason she didn't greet the intruder with a hail of bullets may have been that she was passed out. A pistol was on the floor by her side, and a cartridge clip—but the wrong clip. Dian had had an eye operation the summer before, and her eyesight was bad. Apparently fumbling to load her gun, she had grabbed the wrong clip. Wayne said she had also been suffering from insomnia for the previous two weeks. Maybe with the help of alcohol or pills she had finally sunk into a deep sleep. There was no autopsy. A French doctor came up to do the coroner's report and was so horrified by what he saw that he said there was no need for an autopsy; the cause of death was clear. It would have been useful to have had her blood checked for alcohol, drugs, or poison. With all the tracking expertise in camp, no one thought to track the intruder. Or maybe the tracks didn't lead out of camp. The police came up and took a lot of large, glossy pictures, then launched their African-style investigation.

The next summer, Wayne McGuire was charged with the crime. The American vice consul walked up the mountain to warn Wayne that his arrest was imminent and he should get out of the country. Wayne was reluctant to leave because he felt he was being framed and he hadn't finished the field work for his doctorate. But at the vice consul's urging, he went to Kigali for a few days and flew out of Rwanda on June 27. The police had plenty of opportunity to arrest him on the plane or during the days before the flight, when he was sweating it out in Kigali. But they let him go, and as soon as he left the country an international arrest warrant was issued, charging that he was "suspected of being implicated" in Dian's murder, along with five Rwandans. Four have since been cleared. The fifth, Emmanuel Rwelekana, a tracker who had worked for Dian but was not at Karisoke at the time, reputedly hanged himself in Ruhengeri prison. A government official later described Wayne as the "principal author" of the murder and said that the "presumed motive" was the theft of the scientific research that Dian had accumulated over the years.

On December 11, Wayne was tried *in absentia* in Ruhengeri. The trial lasted twenty-five minutes. One of the few bits of hard evidence presented was that strands of hair found in Dian's clenched hand were tested in France and proved to be from a white person. Wayne was found guilty and sentenced to death by firing squad. The consensus of *mzungu* Karisoke veterans is that Wayne is an innocent scapegoat. Ian Redmond called the charge "nonsense." "The investigation has not been conducted in anything like the way it would have in Europe or the U.S.," he told the press. "Some of the most obvious leads have been ignored. They're concentrating on trying to find someone who is not Rwandan. They feel it looks bad for the country."

Ian said that Wayne had told him, "It's bad enough to be charged with murder, but to be charged with the murder of someone you like is horrible." Amy Vedder told the press that the day after the murder Wayne had seemed "very shaken up . . . confused and shocked. It seemed the behavior of someone who was completely innocent." Others wondered how Wayne could have communicated with his "coconspirators" when he knew only a few words of French and Swahili and was barely able to get through to the staff; like Dian, he was a typically tongue-tied American.

Wayne was safe once he got to America, which doesn't have an extradition treaty with Rwanda. But if the law wasn't after him, the press was. Reporters camped on his parents' lawn in New Jersey, but Wayne, unsure of how to handle this sudden notoriety, dodged them. Eventually he surfaced in Los Angeles with a lawyer and declared his innocence.

In an article published in *Discover* and the London *Sunday Times* that comes across as an affectionate tribute to Dian and a convincing self-exculpation, Wayne explained that charges of theft had arisen from the fact that a few days after the murder, he had passed Dian's cabin and noticed that a window was partly open, and that the guards weren't around. He climbed up to the sill to see if everything was all right and looked in. At that moment two guards came and saw him jumping down. Later the police searched his cabin and found a monthly summary Dian had given him in November, and accused him of stealing it from her cabin. The summary was taken to the *procureur* in Ruhengeri, who confronted Wayne with it, and said it was part of her second book. The report of the condition of the cabin at the time of the murder was later altered to say that everything was there except the manuscript to her second book. Wayne says there was no second book.

"I feel sorry for Dian, and sorry for the gorillas," he concludes. "They may be the unfortunate victims of this sad story." Wayne, too, has suffered. His career has been sidetracked from having to leave the field prematurely and from the inevitable stigma of the accusation. There will always be a shadow of doubt hanging over him: did he or didn't he kill Dian Fossey?

A final possibility is that Dian's murder could have resulted from a simple burglary. In 1981, while she was at Cornell, a burglar broke into her cabin in precisely the same way—by snipping out the tin sheet below her bedroom window—and made off with a camera. The burglar could have tried again five years later. This time Dian was there. The burglar grabbed the nearest weapon—her panga—killed her, and fled in panic without taking anything.

I VISITED DIAN'S grave late one afternoon. She is buried under a circle of stones just above her cabin in a simple pine coffin provided by the American consulate. A postcard picture of her with some gorillas is attached to a wood plaque until the proper headstone arrives from her parents. Around her, with plaques giving their names, are the bodies of gorillas, most of them killed by poachers: Digit; Uncle Bert; Macho; Mwelu, the daughter of Simba and probably Digit, a victim of infanticide by a rival male after the shooting of Uncle Bert, so indirectly also killed by poachers; Kweli, son of Uncle Bert and Macho, who lived three months after being shot; Poppy's child, probably stillborn; Wageni; Marchessa; Frito; Leo; Quince; Nunkie; Kazi; Kurudi. After reading the names, I realized that this is a family plot. This was Dian's family. Schaller had said of her: "I have an empathy for the animals I watch, but to a lesser degree than Dian did, because I have a family. Possibly the gorillas were her real family."

It is David's theory, too, that as she gave up on people the gorillas became surrogate humans for her, and this was the source of her tragedy. There is only so much you can get back from a gorilla. But she had loved them like a mother. Hers was a pure, selfless love, forged in the pain of loneliness, like an artist's love, which doesn't feed or heal your soul, and takes a lot out of you. A damaged, driven person, herself a victim of unlove, she had this extraordinary love, without which there would probably be no gorillas in the Virungas. It was her love that she will be remembered for.

THE LAST OF
THE
DOG-HEADED
MEN

The countryside through the train window could be almost anywhere. The villages dotting it, each clustered around a tall, thin steeple, look French, and the trucks and cars passing along the road below are definitely French—Peugeots, Renaults, the redoubtable Citroën Deux-Chevaux. But they are battered models from ten or twenty years ago, and the earth, bared on slumped, rain-beaten hillsides in the distance, is too red to be European; it is the brick red lateritic soil of the tropics. So this must be some former possession of the French. But where? The passing details are pantropical: a burst of tattered banana leaves, a row of eucalyptus, a mat of water hyacinth, with its striking purple flowers (native to the Amazon, widely introduced because of its attractive purple flower, it now clogs warm waterways around the world), a flock of white egrets shimmering against the slate gray sky. But here, to the right, is a clue, perhaps: a stand of tall sedges with airy round heads—papyrus—establishes that we are somewhere in the Old World tropics; and over there is a grid of shallow pools, with people wading in them—rice paddies. So we are probably in Asia, or on the edge of Asia. Now we are pulling into a station of turn-of-the-century French design: the walls are edged with staggered quoins, a peaked, dormered roof projects over the platform. This could be a stop

in Provence, except that the sign on the station's wall says
AMBOHIMANAMBOLA, and the people milling on the platform,
rushing up to the windows of our car with platters of bananas
and litchi nuts, are not European. They are dark-skinned, tropical people. They aren't African, and they aren't Indian or Ori-
ental, either. They are Afro-Indonesian. Most of them are probably
Merina, the largest and most urban of the eighteen ethnic groups
on Madagascar, who live on the central plateau and in the
nineteenth century conquered the island, and were in turn conquered by the French.

Madagascar. For as long as I can remember, the word has
had a magic ring, has been swathed in visions of the exotic
bordering on the unreal. I remember doing a report when I was
a schoolboy on the coelacanth, a six-foot-long fish that lived in
the Paleozoic era, when fish were starting to grow limbs and
come out on land. It was thought to have been extinct for three
hundred million years, but in 1938 was rediscovered forty fath-
oms down in the waters between Madagascar and the Comoro
Islands, using its paddlelike fins to walk on the ocean floor.
Even at that early age, I had a sense of Madagascar as a lost
world, a huge island out in the Indian Ocean where all kinds
of fantastic holdovers from earlier eras lived on.

It wasn't until I was in my late twenties, researching a book
on the Amazon, that I began to think seriously about taking a
trip to Madagascar. I kept running into strange references to the
island: how a certain genus of stringy, epiphytic cactus, *Rhip-
salis*, is found only in Amazonia, Africa, Ceylon, and on Madagascar; how the closest relative of the seven kinds of Amazon
river turtle was *Erymnochelys madagascariensis*. How could these
two places, halfway around the globe from each other, have such
close evolutionary affinities? The answer, or part of it, is that
long ago South America and Madagascar were both attached to
Africa; they, along with Australia, Antarctica, and India, were

all part of the southern supercontinent, Gondwanaland. Madagascar was up by Tanzania. But then, beginning around a hundred and sixty million years ago, a chunk of Africa broke off and was slowly rafted to its present position, two hundred and fifty miles east of Mozambique. The chunk was a thousand miles from tip to tip and three hundred and fifty miles at its widest point, a minicontinent half again the size of California. ("In shape it resembles the print of a gigantic left foot with an enlarged big toe pointing pigeon-toed slightly to the right of north," Sir Mervyn Brown, Britain's ambassador to the island during the 1970s, wrote in his dry, affectionate history, *Madagascar Rediscovered.*) Meanwhile South America had separated from western Africa and was drifting west. Some ten thousand years ago, during the Pleistocene epoch, Africa suffered widespread desiccation; its forests, which had not been extensive to begin with, shrank and many of their plants and animals were wiped out. But some of the Gondwanaland forms survived on Madagascar and in the Amazon, like the prototypes of the boa constrictor, of which there are many species in the Americas, three on Madagascar, and none in Africa.

By fifty or sixty million years or so ago overland migration between Africa and Madagascar was no longer possible. Cut off from the rest of the world, with no competition from higher, more successful forms of life, the flora and fauna on the island, which was still at a primitive stage of evolution, developed in astonishing ways. A spiny desert that looks like a creation of Dali sprang up in the dry southern part of the island. Trees with bloated, bottlelike trunks for storing water from the infrequent rains (a bizarre adaptation known as crassulescence) proliferated: Madagascar boasts nine species of baobab to Africa's one. The chameleons—lizards that can change color and swivel each eye independently—speciated madly: two-thirds of the world's species, including the world's largest (*Chamaeleo oustaleti*) and the smallest (stubby-tailed *C. nasutus*, scarcely larger than your thumbnail; it plays dead when frightened) hail from Madagascar. The island is the world headquarters not only of chameleons, but of another group, the lemurs—long-snouted, bug-eyed, usually long-tailed, tree-dwelling, squirrel-to-cat-sized prosimians —common ancestors of monkeys, apes, and man. The most intelligent form of life to be stranded on the island, the lemurs filled all sorts of empty niches. Some—the giant lemurs—became grazers, there being no hoofed animals to compete with (hoofed animals had not even evolved yet when Madagascar drifted away); one filled the woodpecker niche, there being no woodpeckers on the island; but most evolved the social behavior and the diurnal, fruit-eating habits of monkeys, there being no higher primates, either. Some forty types of lemur are found on Madagascar, and only there.

The first European naturalists to explore the island were bowled over by the animal and plant life. Philibert Commerson, a Frenchman, declared Madagascar in 1771 "the naturalist's promised land. Nature seems to have retreated there into a private sanctuary, where she could work on different models from any she has used elsewhere. There, you meet bizarre and marvellous forms at every step." The great Victorian natural scientist Alfred Russel Wallace a century later called "this insular subregion . . . one of the most remarkable zoological districts on the globe." As they began to catalogue the flora and fauna they discovered endemic species in numbers unequaled even on the Galápagos. Eighty percent of the flowering plants, of which there are some 8,000 species, are endemic. So are half the 238 bird species. One of the endemic families, the vangas, related to the shrike, has an amazing variety of bill types, like Darwin's finches and the Hawaiian honeycreepers: the helmet vanga has a stout, parrotlike bill; the sickle-billed vanga has a long, thin, decurved probing bill; the coral-billed nuthatch vanga has a sharp, straight nuthatchlike bill with which it stabs insects it finds in bark. As they classified the species and sorted out their relationships, the naturalists discovered that the tremendous diversity on the island had arisen from relatively few models. Some orders are poorly represented; some not at all. There are no vipers—poisonous snakes are a recent development in snake evolution. The only indigenous carnivores are seven peculiar, weaseloid forms of civet cat. Because of the absence of predators, the animals there have a virtual lack of fear. They are incredibly tame. You can walk right up to them.

The human history of Madagascar seems as if it had been made up by someone with an equally wacky imagination. The island was one of the last habitable places on earth to be reached by man. Indonesians sailed in outrigger canoes from the East African coast around A.D. 500, having mixed with the people there as well as with the Dravidians in India earlier in their wanderings. Like the other life forms, the Indonesians experienced an adaptive radiation, settling into the pockets of suitable habitat in the island's immensely varied topography. Those who went into the arid South became herders of cattle and goats (which they must have brought with them). The cattle population of Madagascar is now about even with the human population— eleven million or so—beautiful, sleek zebus that are often more important to their owners as symbols of wealth than as sources of protein. Other Indonesians stayed in the rain forest on the eastern escarpment and became slash-and-burn farmers, irrigated the central plateau and grew paddy rice, or became migratory fishermen, moving up and down the southwest coast, harvesting the teeming life on the reefs. Eventually they all sorted themselves into eighteen ethnic groups, nineteen if you count a shadowy group of hunter-gatherers in the South called the Mikea, who are very small, perhaps actual Pygmies, and sometimes show up in neighboring villages with honey and meat to trade for spears and chewing tobacco, then melt back into the bush. The feet of the Mikea are widely believed to point backwards so they can't be tracked. (Deep in the Amazon forest there is supposed to be a giant called the Curupira, whose feet also point backwards, so there are cultural convergences in the two regions as well.)

Physically the inhabitants of Madagascar, the Malagasies (pronounced the way they are called in French, the *malgaches*), are not all the same people. Those along the coast are generally more African, and those inland more Indonesian. Culturally the Malagasies are essentially Indonesian, but they are a far outlier, a peculiar transplant, the westernmost radiation of Indonesian culture. They all speak the same language, also called Malagasy, or dialects thereof. It is a mellow, polysyllabic tongue whose closest relative is that of the Maanyan of central Borneo. They all farm some kind of rice, paddy or dry, and they are all deeply into ancestor worship, with festive reunions at the family tomb. These are Asian, not African traits, as are the ritual slaughter of cattle practiced by all the ethnic groups, and the Malagasy hut style (rectangular as opposed to round). Their kinship system—loose, ambilateral, no formal clans, but all kinds of relatives (except in parts of the central plateau, where the right to a certain rice paddy is hereditary and genealogies are carefully preserved)—is also typical of an Indo-Pacific island, and unlike the unilineal clan systems that predominate in Africa. Marriages between Malagasies are fluid and easily dissolved. Most Malagasies, if they marry at all, marry several times over their lifetime. The main reason for marrying is to legitimize paternity and to confer respectability on the offspring. There is no dowry or bridewealth, as in Africa, no special ceremony, no exchange of binding vows.

Another important part of the culture are the taboos, or *fady*, which vary from village to village and family to family. A

Merina woman who lived in the capital, Antananarivo, told me that her father's people had a *fady* against eating goat, while her mother's were forbidden to eat chicken cooked with the head and feet, and that it was *fady* on both sides for her to sit on her brother's bed. If she wanted to talk with him, she had to pull up a chair. The *fady* are meant in a positive sense, to keep you out of harm's way.

During the last thousand years Madagascar had growing contacts with Africa. It was probably during this period that the tradition of *tromba*, or spirit possession, and the cult of the *dady*, the dead kings, whose relics—bones, hair, fingernails— are preserved and revered, came to the island, and caught on particularly on the northwest coast. Islamic traders forged a sea route from Zanzibar to the Comoros to the northern part of the island, where they established several thriving trade centers, and that part of the island enjoyed a moment of splendor. It was through the Islamic grapevine that Marco Polo, returning from China in 1294, heard about "the biggest and best [island] in the whole world" (it's actually the fourth biggest, after Greenland, New Guinea, and Borneo; the fifth biggest, if you consider Australia an island and not a continent) and provided the West with its first, largely fanciful account of what, because Polo had confused the island with Mogadishu, a city in Somaliland, came to be known as Madagascar. The island was loaded with elephants, camels, leopards, lynxes, lions, and harts, he reported (again confusing it with the mainland). It also had ostriches of huge size—which was true—the world's largest known birds, *Aepyornis*, related to the rheas of South America, the ostriches of Africa, the emus of Australia, and the moas and kiwis of New Zealand. They became known as elephant birds and were associated with the fabulous rukh of Persian and Arabic legend —half-bird, half-lion, which pounced on elephants, flew up with them to great height, let them go, and then fed on the splattered carcasses. The Great Khan sent an emissary five thousand miles to find out more about the rukh. He was taken captive. A second emissary was dispatched, who freed the first, and they returned with the monstrous tusks of a wild boar.

The Arabs brought slavery, gold money, a taste for luxury, Islam, Swahili, and then, for unknown reasons, they up and left the island to the natives, who were by now at the warring-chiefdom stage of social evolution. Wooden palisades and hill forts with defensive ditches begin to turn up in the archaeological record of this period. There is no prehistoric or historic evidence from Madagascar that gentle, predator-free environments necessarily produce gentle people; and yet the Malagasies are, on the whole, a remarkably serene and a wonderfully polite people. There have been periodic outbreaks of violence on the island but these have been short-lived and seemingly uncharacteristic.

In 1500 the island was sighted by a Portuguese ship that was part of a fleet headed for India and had been blown off course in a storm. Polo's island had been found, and it was up for grabs. In the centuries that followed, the Portuguese, the Dutch, the French, and the British all established footholds on Madagascar. The longest-lived of these was Fort Dauphin, on the southeastern tip, which lasted from 1643 to 1674, when long-festering troubles between the colonists and the natives finally came to a head with the unexpected arrival, due to another storm, of fifteen young women who had been recruited from a French orphanage as brides for the settlers of nearby Réunion. "The stranded girls, fearful of further dangers and privations, begged to be married to some of the settlers on the spot, and La Bretèche [the administrator of the colony] finally agreed," Sir Mervyn Brown writes. "But this news was most unwelcome to the Malagasy women who had been living with the set-tlers. . . . With the fury of women scorned they turned against their lovers and betrayed them to the Malagasy warriors who were ever watchful for an opportunity to attack the settlement." In the middle of the marriage ceremonies, sixty-four of the colonists were massacred. The rest managed to flee to Réunion.

Even the Russians had designs on the island. In 1723 Peter the Great, who decided he needed a sea route to India, sent two warships disguised as trading vessels from the Estonian port of Revel with instructions to seize Madagascar, which he saw as a strategic stop on the way, but one of them sprang a leak as soon as they reached the open sea, and the mission was aborted. By this time an anarchistic pirate utopia called the Republic of Libertalia had been thriving for several decades at Diego Suarez, a magnificent harbor at the northern tip of the island. Libertalia had been set up by the French nobleman Misson and the Italian priest Carracioli, but most of the buccaneers who flocked to it were British—among them legends like Henry Avery and William "Captain" Kidd. Its constitution embraced the latest ideas of the Enlightenment: equal representation, equal division of spoils, and racial equality were guaranteed and slavery was abolished, but as Sir Mervyn pointed out, "there was a basic contradiction in that this philosopher's paradise was sustained economically by the plundering of peaceful merchant ships and the murder of innocent seamen." Nor were its Malagasy neighbors, who eventually destroyed Libertalia in a surprise attack, impressed by its tenet of international brotherhood.

At the end of the eighteenth century, as the Merina were entering the Iron Age, a remarkable leader named Andrianampoinimerina arose among them, and, uniting the chiefdoms of the central plateau, built a splendid palace on a hill within site of the present capital, created a three-tiered society (nobles, free men, slaves), and laid the groundwork for the conquest of the island by his son, Radama I. Andrianampoinimerina's words from his deathbed, in 1810, were so beautiful that they were recorded: "O my eldest son, o fragment of my life, you do not resemble common men; you are like a god fallen on the earth; you are not the issue of my flesh, but come from my mouth, because you are a fruit of the creator. I do not die, I who have a son like you, for you are a beautiful bull. . . ."

Radama's style had none of the austerity of his father, who had gone barefoot and nearly naked, with a white cloth thrown over one shoulder, and a spear in one hand. He dressed like a European monarch and welcomed the English, who helped him conquer the island with guns and military advisers, turned his mind against the French, and sent missionaries from the Society of London to teach his people modern crafts like printing. In a curious echo of the lack of certain orders in the island's flora and fauna, several boxes containing moveable type for printing sank at sea en route to Madagascar when the alphabet was being introduced, and certain letters, most conspicuously *c*, never arrived.

But Radama was very fond of drink and women, and his drunken orgies brought him to an early end. In 1828 he died at the age of only thirty-six, and his dream of bringing Madagascar into the nineteenth century died with him. One of his father's widows, a reactionary, xenophobic woman named Ranavalona, acceded to the throne. Ranavalona renounced the treaty with England, expelled the missionaries and burned at the stake many of the Malagasies who had converted to Christianity. But even as she was purging the island of all things Western, she took as her closest adviser and perhaps lover a Frenchman named Jean Laborde, who had been shipwrecked on the east coast, and who, during the decades he lived in her palace, manufactured cannons, swords, rifles, glass, silk, cement, dyes, ink, soap, tiles, refined sugar, lightning rods, plumbing facilities, wine, rum, and cheese, all from scratch.

Ranavalona's long and repressive rule finally ended with

her death in 1861, and it was the progressive young generation's turn again. The new king, Radama II, restored Christianity and freedom of thought and worship, invited back the missionaries, welcomed European commerce, and abolished the traditional methods of justice, graphically described by Sir Mervyn:

> One method of treating someone suspected of a serious crime [prior to the reign of Radama II] was to cut off first the individual fingers, then the hands, then the limbs until the suspect confessed, when he was instantly executed; so that the poor unfortunate had the choice of being liquidated either at one blow or by installments. More usual was the trial by ordeal using poison derived from the kernel of the fruit of the *tangena* shrub. The accused was made to swallow three pieces of chicken skin and some rice, followed by some scrapings of the *tangena* nut mixed in the juice of a banana. Then large quanties of rice water were drunk to promote vomiting. If all three pieces of skin were vomited up whole the accused was considered innocent.

But all too often the accused failed to regurgitate all three pieces, or died from the effects of the poison after successfully passing the ordeal.

Radama II shared Radama I's fondness for nocturnal debauches, and he surrounded himself with a dissipated young entourage who became known as the *menamaso*, the "red eyes." In 1863 he was strangled by traditionalists in the court, and one of his widows, Rabodo, took the throne, changing her name to Rasoherina (which means "chrysalis") and marrying her prime minister, who lasted only a year before he was replaced by his brother. Her new consort and prime minister, Rainilaiarivony, outlasted her and served the next two queens, Ranavalona II and III, in the same capacity. He was, in effect, the island's absolute ruler for thirty-two years, until it fell to the French. Ranavalona III was the last queen of Madagascar. Her photographs reveal that she was a classic Merina beauty, with the long face and high cheekbones still found among the young women in Antananarivo.

The last years of Merina rule were marked by increasing isolation and rampant corruption. Madagascar's connection with the rest of the world, always tenuous, became even more so after 1869, when the Suez Canal was opened and it was no longer on a major shipping route. In 1895, a French expeditionary force of 14,773 men and 658 officers took the island in spite of stiff resistance from primitively armed natives, and the death of more than half of their numbers from fever. The following year Madagascar became a French overseas territory.

The colonial period was not a happy one. Ancestor-oriented insurrections similar to the Ghost Dance movement that was sweeping the Indians of the American Southwest, who were making their last stand around this time, erupted sporadically until 1904. But within a few years the French had established an intimidating military presence, complete with a loyal Malagasy *garde indigène*, introduced a stable currency, and replaced much of the native forest with plantations of cloves, coffee, tobacco, cocoa, sisal, and eucalyptus. By 1905, thanks to the superhuman efforts of native laborers with French administrators in pith helmets and jodhpurs standing by, cracking riding crops on their thighs (a familiar presence on the island as late as 1973), a railroad had been completed from Antananarivo to the east coast. By 1914 Madagascar had been brought sufficiently into the imperial fold that 45,863 of her young men were drafted into the French colonial infantry and shipped off to the Great War, to cover themselves with glory on the fields of combat. Four thousand of them bled or froze to death, were gassed, blown up, or cut down in the trenches.

The postwar period began as a time of relative prosperity. Bridges and roads were built, more track was laid. Between 1924 and 1932 the number of cars on the island doubled to sixty-five hundred. On December 17, 1932, the first "Micheline," or bus on rails, arrived in Antananarivo, and a swarm of linen-suited colonials and *évolués* was on hand to greet it. But 1932 was perhaps the high-water mark of the colonial period. There was a slight lag before the economic crisis from which the Northern Hemisphere was reeling hit the island, then the rest of the thirties were as grim for the Malagasies as they were for everybody. Marginally important colonies like Madagascar were more or less left to fend for themselves, and the close of the decade saw a rise of newfound nationalism. There was a huge rally in the capital as Ranavalona III's ashes were finally allowed to return to the island.

Few Malagasies or even French administrators were aware of the Third Reich's Madagascar Plan, a grotesque codex to the history of this period. As early as 1934 Hitler toyed with the idea of forcibly deporting the Jews in Europe to Madagascar. The so-called Madagascar Plan was taken seriously. Eichmann worked on the details full-time for a year, surrounding himself with maritime experts, lining up ships on the North German Lloyd and Hamburg-American lines that would transport four million Jews to the island (they would of course have to pay their own passage), where it was hoped they would all die a slow death from tropical diseases. Mussolini thought the plan was a great idea. So did Himmler, but Goebbels lobbied for extermination. In May, 1942, when the plan was still under consideration, the British, pretending to be going to Antarctica so De Gaulle wouldn't discover their real mission, took the northern part of the island from the Vichy government in a spectacular naval action. The British interest in Madagascar was to keep the Japanese from getting it, but with the island now in their hands, the Madagascar Plan was dropped. Several months later, Hitler settled on the Final Solution.

After the war France attempted to continue the colonial system, and the Malagasies, like many in French Africa, became increasingly restive. In 1947 a bloody rebellion broke out on the eastern escarpment and was put down with the help of African troops stationed on the island. "The Sénégalais and the Moroccans killed many of us," a Malagasy told me. "Then it was us the French used against the Algerians and the Vietnamese. *C'est ça le système colonial.*" It was the Algerians who sprung everybody. In 1960 De Gaulle declared that the empire had ended, and Malagasy was independent, but only nominally. The Première République, the Malagasy Republic, was a pro-French, neocolonial affair. Pith-helmeted administrators were still in charge.

Almost everyone on Madagascar by now is aware that he or she is part of a national experiment, although many are still governed more by local custom than by the *pouvoir révolutionnaire* that emanates from the capital. Recently a team of botanists from the Missouri Botanical Garden, while exploring the virgin rain forest on the Masoala peninsula on the east coast (where they discovered two genera of palm unknown to science), ran into people who had never seen a motor vehicle. In 1972 fifty-five percent of the Malagasies were still "animists"; they still practiced traditional ancestor worship and believed that they would turn into crocodiles, boas, or lemurs when they died. The balance were Christians, with a fifty-fifty split between Catholics and Protestants, the Catholics being in the French camp, "toadies of the colonials," one man told me, while the revolutionaries were invariably Protestant. It was Protestants who started the trouble at the School of Medicine in 1972. Against a backdrop of mounting economic problems and the greater issue of whether to remain a servant-state of France, the medical students went

on strike. There had been a long tradition of resistance at the
School of Medicine. Students there had founded a secret rev-
olutionary society as early as 1913. The school was run by
France but its graduates didn't receive European accreditation;
they became "bush" doctors, black doctors. The students wanted
to be real doctors. The strike led to huge demonstrations in the
capital, which brought down the Première République. The
xenophobic, Marxist Deuxième République, the Democratic Republic of Madagascar, was formed. The president resigned and
was replaced by a left-leaning general who was unable to establish unity and was replaced by the radically left-wing Colonel
Richard Ratsimandrava, who lasted only three days. Ratsimandrava was being driven from the presidential palace to his residence in a military compound when the chauffeur slowed down
for a hole in the road, and three men with machine guns jumped
out of a utility van and blew him and his driver and bodyguards
away; who the assassins were or why they did it has never been
determined. He was succeeded by the current president, his
archrival, a navy captain named Didier Ratsiraka, who continued his policy of *socialisme méfiant* and developed a strong
rapport with the Eastern bloc, buddying up to countries like
Rumania, Cuba, North Korea. (I remember pulling up in my
rented car to one of the wide *prospekts* in Leningrad in the fall
of 1979—I was on the way to meet a long-lost cousin at the
Conservatory of Music—and being detained by an amazing high-
speed motorcade. First fifty little Zhigouli sedans streaked by
in formation, doing about fifty miles an hour. Then fifty mid-
sized Volgas, then fifty big Chaikas, with tail fins and chrome
lateral lines obviously inspired by the 1956 Ford Fairlane, then
a diamond of yellow motorcycles, maybe a hundred of them.
Inside the diamond was a huge stretch limo, with the curtains
drawn, and inside the limo, I read in *Pravda* the next day, were
the head of the Leningrad Soviet, Vladimir Romanov [no relation

to the tsars], and Didier Ratsiraka, the president of Madagascar. Then, in descending order, more formations of Chaikas, Volgas, and Zhigoulis.)

About three years ago there was a marked shift in the Deuxième République's foreign policy. Global recession and inflation were having a devastating impact on the Third World. The market for Madagascar's exports—vanilla, cloves, coffee, sisal, graphite—was drying up; the total earnings from them weren't even enough to cover the interest on the foreign debt. The GNP was slipping precipitously, per capita income had dropped twenty-five percent since 1979, basic necessities were unavailable (we would be besieged with requests for malaria pills, soap, pens, paper, offers for the jogging shoes and the shirts we had on). There was a match crunch, a *pénurie d'allumettes*. Malagasy matches had not been produced for some time (not that they were any good—only one of every three struck ignited) and the island was running out of the Double Happiness matches it imported from Red China; in some towns there wasn't a match to be had. Spare parts for cars and trucks were even scarcer; the colonial road system was reverting to the wild; the young generation of Malagasies, eager to make its mark, was *bloquée*; there would be, before and after our visit, food riots and looting sprees, the situation was the worst it had been since independence. Clearly, aligning with the Eastern bloc, whose only contributions had been useless *grande idéologie* and some military matériel, was a *politique mal orientée*. More free enterprise and fewer socialistic constraints, more of the West's technology and development strategies were needed. While trying to hurt as few feelings as possible, President Ratsiraka, like the heads of many of the developing nations, placed himself under the paternalistic protection, the self-interested largesse, of the Western powers, allowing agencies like the International Monetary Fund and the World Bank to become a sort of *superétat*.

On top of and compounding its economic problems, Madagascar is on the brink of environmental catastrophe. After centuries of deforestation, the island is self-destructing, washing into the sea, going the way of Haiti and the Sahel. Huge gashes of eroded red earth are such a characteristic feature of its landscapes that there is a special word for them in Malagasy, *lavaka*. A recent study by the World Wildlife Fund has determined that Madagascar is the most eroded place on earth: two million acres a year are being lost to erosion, about four-fifths of the island is already barren, burnt-over, brick-hard, sun-baked laterite. The destruction has been going on, of course, since prehistoric times. The largest of Madagascar's animals were already gone before any European got a chance to see them: the giant lemurs, the pygmy hippopotamus (which probably swam over from Africa during the Pleistocene); the elephant bird, one of whose eggs provided an omelette for fifty people, went the way of the dodo on nearby Mauritius and the moa on New Zealand, but without European help. In all, sixteen genera of vertebrates have gone extinct on Madagascar since humans arrived. Islands go a lot faster than mainlands do because they are smaller and the minimum critical habitats of their species are disturbed more quickly, and because a lot of the species aren't adapted to predation; flightless birds, for instance, are helpless against introduced terrestrial mammals like pigs, dogs, rats, mongooses, and man.

With eighty percent of Malagasies still living off the land, there is tremendous pressure on the last remaining tracts of forest for space to grow food, timber, charcoal, and pasture. The people are in a terrible bind: as the ecologist Alison Jolly, who has been working on Madagascar for twenty-five years, and her husband Richard Jolly, an economist with UNICEF, have put it, the Malagasies are being forced to sacrifice their future so that they can survive in the present; they are caught in a "tragedy without villains." Most of them aren't aware of the consequences

·

of what they are doing; unless they are stopped there will soon be nothing left, and a food crisis like the one that is taking millions of lives right across the channel in Mozambique will set in.

The last good survey, completed twenty-five years ago, estimated that only twenty-one percent of the original forest, which is thought by some to have blanketed almost the entire island, remained. Recent satellite photos suggested that only half of those patches are standing today, and a 1981 project by the United Nations' Food and Agricultural Organization determined that thirty percent of the present forest will be gone by the year 2000. Because of the island's unequaled levels of endemism (more than ninety-five percent of its reptiles, 148 of the 150 frogs, to continue the list, are not found anywhere else in the world), clearing a patch of forest on Madagascar has more devastating repercussions than probably anywhere. And many of the things haven't even been identified yet. "Entire mountain massifs and river basins have never had a botanist in them," the botanist Peter Lowrie, who was on the expedition that found the two new genera of palm, told me. "It's one of the truly underexplored areas in the world."

Late in 1984, the government, prodded by foreign scientists, enacted a new program, a *Stratégie de la Conservation et du Développement Durable*, but the problem was money. Madagascar has an excellent park system on paper. Set up by the French in 1927, it was one of the first in the African region, but its thirty-six national parks and reserves protect only one percent of the island, and that only theoretically, as poaching of timber and wildlife in them is virtually unchecked; the entire annual budget for maintaining the system is only a thousand dollars. So in this matter, too, the government has looked to the West; it has entrusted nothing less than the salvation of the island to agencies like the World Wildlife Fund, which now considers Madagascar the highest conservation priority in the world. "We're identifying critical areas, shoring up local institutions and creating new ones, sending Malagasy graduate students to the States for training, educating the local people and getting them involved in antipoaching," Thomas Lovejoy, who is overseeing the fund's work on the island, told me. "All islands have a peculiar intensity," he went on. "They are self-contained worlds that lend themselves as microcosms. It is easier to trace the fates of the limited number of life forms that are turned loose on them. This great red island Madagascar is particularly fascinating not only because so many of its forms are unique, but because the whole drama of human aspirations in the tropics is being played out on it."

In some ways, Lovejoy told me, it was an exciting era. Many things that had been impossible under the Deuxième République were now do-able. Scientific permits were being issued to foreigners without delay, and in 1985 a thirteen-year ban on tourism was lifted and tourists were beginning to come to the island. They tended to be young, adventurous Europeans, a woman in the division of tourism told me, who were looking for *"quelquechose de primitif."* The American market was completely untapped, she said. So we were the vanguard.

THE TRAIN FOLLOWED the old line from the capital to the coast, and it was nicknamed Fandrefiala, after a forest snake, because it snaked through the forest. But we had been on it several hours and we still hadn't seen any forest, only manmade grassland. We limped along, stopping frequently. Twice we changed engines. It was January—the cyclone season. There had been heavy rains the last few days, and in several places rivers had risen almost over the tracks. The day before a man in the capital had told me that once during the cyclone season he had been stuck for several days on this train. He had made himself a hammock in the luggage rack, and people from the nearest village, which had been flooded, had come and slept on the train until the waters subsided.

My sons André and Nicky had made friends with some other kids on the train, and they were wowing them with their little plastic double-transformer Autobots, which change from robots into trucks. I was glad to have them along, partly for selfish reasons—I didn't like to be away from them, and they made my work easier, they broke the ice for me—and partly because I wanted them to see lemurs in the wild while there were still some to be seen. They were already, at the ages of eight and six, seasoned travelers, regular little troupers. They had sat with mountain gorillas in Rwanda and ridden horses behind Navajos and Havasupais into the gaping canyons of the Southwest. They asked good questions.

Michel Rakotonirina, who was in charge of special tourism on the island—Boy Scouts, scientists—had come along with us to see that there were no problems. He bought us some litchis, and we tore open their pimpled red pericarps and popped their translucent white flesh into our mouths. They were a hundred times more ambrosial than the canned litchis one gets in Chinese restaurants. I asked Michel what we were going to do at Perinet, a little town on the eastern escarpment that we were scheduled to reach at noon. "This is where you go to experience the indri," he said. "The indri is the largest of the lemurs. The people around Perinet believe that it is their ancestor." Perinet was said to be a naturalist's paradise. Twenty-six years ago, in a charming book called *Bridge to the Past*, David Attenborough wrote of his visit there. Attenborough was then a young filmmaker who was shooting natural history movies for the BBC—he had not yet made it big with his "Life on Earth" series—and his guide was Michel Rakotonirina, then a young forester at Perinet.

At about ten o'clock—we had left Antananarivo at five-thirty—we finally reached the limit of the denuded grassland. The train began to weave in and out of gorges where there were still, alternating with charred, smoldering clearings, remnants of one of the southernmost rain forests in the world—tall trees with purple flowers, magnificent tree ferns. At eleven we pulled into Moramanga, one of the hot points of the 1947 rebellion. That year, on the night of March 29, two thousand Malagasies, armed with spears, axes, and machetes, had attacked the military camp here. The surviving Sénégalais had retaliated by sowing death in the nearby villages, and in the ensuing turmoil stores were looted and burned, whites were killed, ancient tribal enmities were rekindled, and the old precolonial flag, with eighteen stars symbolizing the ethnic groups, was raised. Villagers were recruited by sorcerers who promised that the guns of the French would discharge only water and that America would come to their assistance. La Rébellion des Sagaies (Spears) lasted until December 1 of the following year. Eleven thousand people died in it. News of the insurrection wasn't allowed to leave the island, lest it give ideas to the other colonies.

The next stop—by now we were in thick jungle—was Perinet, named after a French engineer who died during the construction of the railroad. Here there were a few hundred yards of double track, so that the daily trains from the capital and from the coast could pass each other before continuing on their respective journeys. If all went well, this maneuver usually happened around lunchtime, but sometimes one of the trains would be delayed, and the other would have to wait. There were rooms and a restaurant at the Hotel-Buffet de la Gare, a large, rambling station of the same architecture as the other stations on the line. Porters took our bags as we stepped off the train and we shook hands with the keeper of the hotel, Joseph Adrianjaka, who led us through a small crowd of the halt and lame thrusting out their hands at the entrance, and up a grand rosewood staircase to our room. We washed up and came right down for lunch. The restaurant was a large room with thick posts and beams of rosewood that Joseph said had been cut in the forest in 1943 and would cost a fortune now. He introduced his wife and children. Two of them were boys, who became André and Nicky's pals, took them to their school and to the swimming hole, and taught them dominoes. Joseph and I also spent a lot of time together—we were the only guests—walking in the village, listening in the evening to records of Big Bill Broonzy and Black Orpheus he had from his student days, talking about what he called "the form of life." He said that he had read everything Tolstoy had ever written. He was a gentle man of thirty-eight, with an almost feline grace, and I was forty; we were both in the middle of our respective plays, as he put it. He had been running the hotel for fifteen years. His predecessor was described marvelously by Attenborough, who arrived at Perinet in a Land-Rover and, surprised to find such a large hotel in the middle of nowhere, entered. "Our footsteps echoed with embarrassing loudness on the polished wooden floor. We coughed apologetically once or twice." At last a door opened and "an extremely glamorous girl," wearing only a "flimsy silk housecoat that barely succeeded in covering her ample figure," came out. The woman, Attenborough eventually learned, had been obliged to leave the capital because of a *grand scandale*.

Lunch was the national dish, manioc leaves with pork on rice. The beer, Four Horses, was great (I have never been in a tropical country where it wasn't). In the days that followed, Joseph served up one superb meal after another: kabob with saffron rice, followed by banana *flambé*; braised goose; a delicate, white, slightly fishy meat that turned out to be eel from the creek behind the hotel—enormous eel, four inches in diameter. The food was prepared on glowing charcoal braziers in a cavernous kitchen with soot-blackened walls, where several women were usually singing as they diced carrots beside the sink, and children and chickens were constantly wandering in.

After lunch a slim young man in rubber boots who had been waiting meekly at the door with his hat in his hands came over and introduced himself. His name was Maurice Ratsizakanana, and he was the nineteen-year-old son of the forester of the Analamaotra-Perinet reserve. He said if we were interested he could take us to see the indri. I looked up at the sky. It was dark, and there was a tension in the air, as if at any minute it were going to start pouring. The eastern escarpment gets about a foot of rain in January. "What about our ponchos?" I asked. Maurice said it wasn't going to rain for a couple of hours, but it wouldn't hurt to take them along, so I got them and we set out on the road behind the hotel, which he said was Ancienne Route Nationale Numéro Deux.

The road went through a forest teeming with bird song and frog and insect din. A large black parrot, one of the endemic species, flew over us, calling on the wing—three descending notes. To our left a muddy creek ran through the trees, one of which was leaning out over the water and was dripping with tightly coiled scarlet flowers that looked just like holly berries; the genus of the tree, *Symphonia*, is also represented in the New World. Several large, iridescent moths were hovering over the flowers, their swallow-tailed wings a blurred flurry of black, green, red, white, and blue. They were the famous day-flying moths, *Chrysiridia madagascariensis*. I had seen their relative in the Amazon, which is spectacular, but these moths were larger and even more magnificently colored. "Totally awesome," André declared. The iridescence of their wings, like the iridescence of rainbows, oil slicks, soap bubbles, and corned beef, is structural, rather than pigmental; it is caused by a series of overlapping films on the wall of each scale. Each film is of submicroscopic thickness and has a different refractive index, so it picks up a different color from the light that strikes it. Some years the *Chrysiridia*s migrate over the island in clouds of tens of thousands.

The forest around Perinet was full of butterflies, especially in the morning, when the sun was out. More than three thousand species of butterfly and moth have been described from Madagascar so far, and ninety-seven percent of them are endemic. No one has even studied the smaller species, the Lycaenidae and the Satyridae families. The Malagasies call some butterflies *lolopaty*, which means "spirits of the dead." On some parts of the island the insects are believed to be reincarnations of people. The word for the *Chrysiridia* moth is *lolonandriana*, "noble spirit."

Down the road we came upon one of Madagascar's botanical wonders, a traveler's palm, *Ravenala madagascariensis*, whose slender trunk shot up twenty-five feet, then produced a stately fan of huge bananalike leaves (the tree is actually in the banana family). The reserve was on the left. It had been created in 1970 and there were only eighteen square miles in it, Maurice said. He led us past a fish farm, where his father was raising Nile perch, and up a steep path to a ridge, one of the ridges, with deep, moist glades between them, which pleat the eastern escarpment.

The trees on the ridge were short and twisted, encrusted and festooned with ferns, orchids, lichens, mushrooms. Many of the plants beneath them were recognizable in a general way—as club mosses, as maidenhair ferns, as mimosas, as members of the Melastoma family (the leaves of melastomes have pinnately netted veins and are unmistakable, once you have seen a few of them), and the overall physiognomy of the woods was familiar. This was high jungle, a variation on a theme I had seen stated in many different ways in Africa and South America. I had a sense not so much of being somewhere new and strange, as of being back in a world that I knew, and I felt alive, engaged in a way that I had not felt since the last time I had been in a rain forest.

Passing through a patch of cicada din—the drone of the insects was deafening when we were right among them, but it faded away within a dozen yards—we came to several tall wire-mesh structures. An unsuccessful attempt to keep indri in captivity, Maurice explained. It hadn't been clear whether it was the bananas or being in cages that the indri hadn't liked, but they had refused to eat, and had to be released. Indri eat the fruit and leaves of some sixty trees. "There is a family of them up on this ridge," Maurice said. "In the morning they sing, they tell you exactly where they are, so it is easy to find them. But they stop singing at about two o'clock, so it may take a while to find them. You wait here, while I go look."

The boys chased wood nymphs—little brown butterflies with orange and black eyespots—dancing in the path. Their mom had made them butterfly nets from an old gauze curtain. Michel, who had come with us, found a paradise flycatcher, a small brown bird with long flaming blue streamer tails, sitting on a nest about four feet from the ground. The bird was amazingly tame, letting me approach within a few feet and take its picture. After a while it hopped off the nest, and up popped four tiny, wide open, noiselessly clamoring mouths. I wondered if their father or an older brother had been keeping them warm. Some male birds prefer to help with their mother's next broods than to have children of their own.

We watched a ten-inch green chameleon (the boys thought it was a "comedian") creep ever so slowly down a branch, with its tail wrapped around the branch to keep from falling. Several times it stopped and did a quick, nervous push-up, and rotated its bulging eyes in different directions. "He's very patient," Michel said. Suddenly it shot out its tongue—a pink laser as long as its body, that had been coiled in the back of its throat —and picked off a bug from a nearby leaf.

Twenty-six years earlier the indri had been very hard to get a look at. Attenborough had heard their "deafening eerie wail" once, then for six days he had heard nothing, and he had been unable to find a trace of them. Some days (weather and temperature seem to be factors), the indri don't sing at all, but on seventy percent of the days of the year, they do sing, from one to seven times. A single song lasts from forty seconds to four minutes. On the seventh day Attenborough heard their "stentorian trumpeting" again, and rushing to where the sound was coming from, he got there in time to catch a "momentary glimpse of a body sailing through the air." It was only by playing their song, which he tape-recorded, back to them, that he finally got them to hold, indignant, fascinated.

Over 1972–73 a young British scientist named J. E. Pollock spent ten months observing eight groups of indri. Two of them became so used to his presence that they would approach and feed within fifteen feet of him. Most of what is known about the animal was picked up by Pollock. He learned that the groups are nuclear families—a mother, father, and two or three young—but didn't find out whether the parents mate for life, or if they ever have other partners. The children come only every three years or so (which is an indication of low predator pressure). Each family has its own fixed territory. At night the members sleep on pallets of leaves they make thirty to a hundred feet up in trees, no more than two together. After waking and stretching, and urinating and defecating in concert, they all set out on their feeding route, moving from tree to tree. Pollock found evidence of "persistent female dominance"; the females would lead the group into the next tree, and "only they appeared to succeed in freely and independently moving and feeding," while the males hung back until they had eaten their fill. At first Pollock thought the males were performing some kind of lookout function, but he eventually concluded that he was witnessing "social displacement"—the males withdrawing so the females could feed without hindrance or competition. He also saw the males make sexual overtures to the females and repeatedly be rejected "with a cuff or a violent shrugging action, causing the male to immediately dismount." This is very strange behavior for primates. In most species, like chimpanzees, gorillas, and spider monkeys, the males are bigger and stronger, and they have the pick of food and females. Perhaps, Pollock conjectured, the female dominance of the indri is a function of their being committed monogamists. Perhaps it is "more to the male's advantage to foster development of the infant and invest in the health of the adult female . . . than if his paternity was in doubt."

After about fifteen minutes Maurice came running. "Quick," he said, "I found the indri," and we hurried after him. Suddenly we were stopped in our tracks by an unearthly, spine-chilling, incredibly loud braying and hooting up in the trees maybe a hundred yards ahead. I fumbled for the tape recorder in my sidebag but by the time I got it out they had stopped. Maurice led us to the edge of the ridge and there they were—four creatures with the bodies of monkeys and the faces of dogs and the black and white fur of pandas, with bare black muzzles and rust on the tummy—making their way through some trees, one after another. Attenborough proposed that the indri was the inspiration of the cynocephalus—the fabled dog-headed man who graced the pages of sixteenth-century natural histories, along with dragons, manticores, hydras, and unicorns. These ones seemed to be in no hurry, to be used to being watched.

The great mystery about the indri is why they have no tails. Primates are only supposed to lose their tails when they come down from the trees, and the indri are still arboreal. In compensation they rely on incredibly powerful and agile legs and arms for balance and support. One of them pushed off from a tree with an explosive straightening of its legs and, keeping its body erect, landed against another tree maybe fifteen feet away. It gripped with its feet, then bounced to another tree, ricocheted off that one, and finally came to rest in a fourth tree. The whole leaping sequence took no more than a few seconds.

The song of the indri is one of the loudest sounds made by any animal. It carries more than a mile. Pollock described it as "a relaxed event": the indri simply raise their muzzles into the air and cut loose. He speculated that it serves as a "mechanism of self-advertisement essential for territorial defense," and that it may also convey information about the presence of danger, the discovery of food, and the location and the sexual availability of individuals in the group. Howler monkeys in the New World and gibbons on Borneo have similar songs.

Hoping they would sing again, I got my tape recorder ready, but by accident, trying to get to clean tape, I cut into a recording I had made the day before of three children singing in a street in Antananarivo. The indri snapped to attention. Cocking their heads, pricking up their Teddy-bear ears, they hissed anxiously to each other, then glared down at us with their sparkling yellow eyes, and, opening their small, brilliant-red mouths, they let out a chilling volley of raw barks, of peacocklike squawks— *leur cri dérangé*, Maurice explained. They were upset, but they were also intrigued. They lingered for a half hour or so, waiting for something else to happen, for some other communication from across the vast evolutionary distance between us.

S. Dillon Ripley, the emeritus secretary of the Smithsonian Institution, has described the lemurs as "the first animals you think might have a soul," but it was my impression that there wasn't a whole lot going on behind their big, bright eyes. The kinship I felt with them was remote. (With other primates I have encountered in the wild—howler monkeys, spider monkeys, mountain gorillas—I have felt that I could strike up a conversation if I only knew the language.) Much of the time Pollock observed the indri they remained "virtually immobile," sleeping or digesting leaves in their voluminous viscera. Some days they were active for only five hours. Social interactions, such as grooming each other, which play such an important part in the lives of the higher primates, took up only two percent of their activity period.

At last the indri moved on, and we descended the ridge into a beautiful glade with a stream running through it, which we crossed on a huge fallen tree provided with handrails. Maurice pointed out a malachite kingfisher perched vigilantly over the stream. A large swallowtail with luminous green wing bars came up the stream bed—one of the island's rare endemics, *Papilio mangoura*, which European and American butterfly collectors pay big money for—and, darting among gigantic tree ferns, disappeared into a bamboo glade. As we waded through wet knee-high grass I noticed that a brown inchworm, about three-quarters of an inch long, had landed on the back of my hand. I tried to flick it off, but its head was fastened to my skin. Maurice said it was a *sangsue*, a bloodsucker. I had seen water leeches but nothing like this. The inchwormlike land leech is an Asian form—common in places like Ceylon, Borneo, Vietnam, and Australia, and not found in the New World. There are certain places in New Guinea where one allegedly can be exsanguinated by these leeches in a couple of hours. This was the only place we ran into them, but it was thick with them. When we got out of the grass we inspected each other and found that each of us had half a dozen on him. They were very aggressive. They had punched holes through our socks, come in through the ventilation holes and shoelace eyelets of our sneakers; Nicky had one on the back of his neck. It was important to get them off before they embedded themselves too deeply. They seemed to be ravenous, perhaps because there were so few warm-blooded mammals for them to feed on—only rodents, tenrecs (small, primitive insectivores with hedgehoglike quills), and the occasional human. A meal can last them a whole year. The wounds they made were aseptic and bled freely, because the leeches secrete an antibiotic along with an anticoagulant substance called hirudin, which keeps the blood flowing. Maurice picked a plant, a composite herb in the genus *Ageratum*, crushed it in his hands, and dripped its juice onto our wounds. It stopped the bleeding.

We followed the stream to an open place where it and another stream were backed up in a small pond by a dam. The pungent smell of the grass and the herbs and the red earth around the dam were strangely familiar. For a moment I was overwhelmed by powerful emotions that the odor called forth. It took a moment to recognize the smell as that of the savanna of central Brazil, the cerrado, which I had spent hours exploring one spring ten years earlier. To think that I had been carrying around this smell with me and hadn't known it. So there were olfactory convergences among the earth's various tropical regions as well.

We had one more encounter—with a large bird standing in the path fifty yards ahead; the bird took off and sailed on ghostly white wings into some *Casuarina* trees—then it started to pour—a real deluge. We dashed to the forester's hut, where we found Maurice's father, Jaosolo Besoa, a small man with a mischievous air, in orange rubber boots and green fatigues over a white shirt and tie. Jaosolo had been a forester in the Direction des Eaux et Forêts for twenty years. The bird we had just seen, he said, was a crested ibis. "It is in the process of disappearing because it is hunted by poachers. It is *très rare, monsieur*. Only found on the coasts. It eats ants. That is what it was doing in the path. We call it the *akouanala*, or vampire." We talked about the indri, which the Malagasies call *babakoto*, or grand-father. *Indri* actually means "look at that" in Malagasy. The first European to give an account of the animal, a Frenchman named Sonneret in 1782, reported that its name was indri. One imagines Sonneret's guides pointing one out to him and exclaiming, "In-dri, indri." Sonneret also reported that the indri "cries like a child."

"People here think they are the *babakoto*'s sons, so they don't eat him," Jaosolo told us. "He cries from seven to one o'clock, most often twice, at nine and eleven. The song is a rallying cry, a cry of greeting for all of the groups." According to local legend, Jaosolo went on, "the *babakoto* circumcise their newborn, the way people do. The mother sets a day for the circumcision and invites the neighboring groups to the cere-mony, then she waits with her baby on a branch for them to arrive. Before birds or men are stirring the father goes to the river and drinks up a mouthful of water to wash the wound. Someone from one of the invited groups performs the operation, cutting the foreskin with his fingernail, and finally tearing it off with his teeth. Afterward the father takes the body and tosses it to the mother, and if it falls to the ground, it is left to die. They all take off, because if the baby can't cling to the mother's stomach, it is thought to be sick." Attenborough had picked up the same story about the mother and father tossing the infant back and forth. He was also told that the indri act as watchdogs for the villagers and howl at the approach of thieves. Jaosolo said that when someone was building a house the *babakoto* would come and watch. I asked how the local people had come to believe the *babakoto* was their ancestor. "I don't know," he said. "But it's logical."

It rained so hard that night the water lines to the hotel were washed out, and water had to be heated in the kitchen and brought up to our rooms in buckets for us to bathe. Joseph and I stayed up in the restaurant listening to his nephew sing mellow Malagasy ballads, accompanying himself on the guitar in an American Travis-picking style. He did a beautiful version in his own tongue of Arlo Guthrie's "The City of New Orleans." American country music reached Madagascar via France in the early seventies, and "it immediately struck a chord with our romantic, melancholic temperament," Joseph told me.

Joseph said that he had been studying different religions, trying to find the common line between them, and his conclusion was that "You don't have to be a *savant. C'est en vous.*" We talked about the Hindu and Buddhist notion that the outer, visible world is an illusion. "There is a lot of truth to this notion," Joseph said. "We have an expression, *nifanahy nomaha uluna, c'est l'esprit qui fait l'homme.* It's what you can't see in the person that is his principal constituent. Shakespeare says the same thing: the world is *une scène de théatre,* and each person is an actor. But the true form of life, what is really happening, I think, is that we are living was what lived before. All religions speak of this, but the best version I know of is in Solomon. Every two or three thousand years there is a consummation of energy, then there is *le déluge* (except this time it looks like it's going to be *une explosion atomique*) and everything on earth is destroyed, but not the earth itself. For two or three thousand years the earth is devoid of life, then life regenerates and begins again. I'm afraid there are unmistakable signs that the saturation point is being reached again. This is my personal view." I didn't want to ask him how much time he thinks Madagascar has before it blows, so I said there were definite signs that the saturation point was being reached in my part of the world. Then I thought, how reasonable a cyclical flood theory seemed here in the middle of the rain forest, in the middle of the rainy season, when the days begin clear and sunny, and as they go on the air becomes increasingly heavy and congested, wispy puffs and swirls of vapor swell up into mountainous clouds of cumulonimbus that crowd out the blue and finally let go with *le déluge*. I remembered a song a woman in the Johncrow Mountains of Jamaica had once sung for me: "In the morning I rise up singing / In the evening I wither away / Get ready everybody, get ready / Get ready for the judgment day." "Do you really think that's what we're in for?" I asked Joseph, and for a long time we were silent.

After a six-thirty breakfast of café au lait, bread, and jam, we set out with Maurice again. Michel, assured I was in good hands, stayed behind, waiting for the train to Antananarivo. The whole population seemed to be on the road—the men with axes and brush hooks and bundles on sticks slung over their shoulders, hobo-style, the women with baskets of manioc leaves, sweet potato leaves, breadfruit, or Chinese lettuce on their heads, to sell at the market in town—greeting us gaily as they passed. The greeting here was *Salaam*—God be with you—much as Swiss peasants in the Bernese Oberland say *Grüssgott*, while Bahutu farmers in Rwanda take both your hands and give you a hearty *Mwaramutseho*.

The swollen creek, sliding through the trees, was about eight feet higher than it had been yesterday. The log bridge we had crossed was under water because, Maurice told us, the dam where I had smelled the smell of the Brazilian cerrado had been washed out. Indri were calling in the distance—a sad, beautiful sound, like the song of the humpback whale, or the wail of a loon. That morning we saw more kinds of birds than I had ever seen in a single outing; they were so unfazed and obliging you to walk right up to them. Among the ones we identified were blue couas, opalescent green doves, magpie robins, rollers, vermilion foudias, sunbirds, drongos, warblers, forest kingfishers, rails, honeycreepers, cuckoo shrikes, blue vangas, and bulbuls. Seventy species have been identified in the preserve, but there must be more. I decided to give my binoculars to Maurice. Small, six-by-eighteen Nixons, I'd had them for ten years, and they had brought me closer to thousands of birds on four continents: azure tits in Novgorod, fish eagles on Lake Idi Amin Dada, red-bellied woodpeckers in Westchester County, hyacinthine macaws in the Pantanal do Mato Grosso. "This is one of my oldest and best friends," I said to him, draping the binoculars around his neck. "If you're going to become a great guide you're going to need them." Maurice was overcome. Tears gathered in his eyes and he said, "This is a day I will never forget, monsieur." The next day he asked me to give him a note in case the police accused him of stealing them.

Maurice led us through the knee-deep water of the flooded creek to see a sacred tree. It has a name, *kakuzotsi fantata*, which he told us means the tree whose name nobody knows. It was the tallest, oldest tree in the forest, he said as we stood beneath it and looked up to its crown, some sixty feet above us. It was crowded by other, lower trees, cabled with lianas, and partly wrapped in the embrace of a strangler fig, so it was hard to tell which were its leaves. I borrowed the binoculars and after some time made out small and simple leaves—and that was as far as I could get identifying them. Nobody—not the old locals who knew every tree in the forest, not the *vazaha* (white in Malagasy) botanists from universities in Europe, had succeeded in figuring out what tree it was, Maurice said. Later his father told us, "The first branch is like *Dalbergia* (rosewood). The second is like *Breonia*. In 1963 a sorcerer named Pétain tried to take part of the tree and he would have died if he hadn't sacrificed a cow to the tree, as he was told to do in a dream. Then the forester before me tried to take a cutting of the tree and he died that night." People came and danced under the tree, slaughtered goats, left offerings of money, rum, and candy, he said—women who weren't getting pregnant, men who weren't having luck in love, people who wanted to get rich, students who wanted an *admissible* on their exams. Throughout Madagascar venerable trees and prominent rocks are commonly the site of observances having to do with ancestors. They are thought to be inhabited by a special category of spirits known as *togny*, who are associated with the *hasina*, the most sacred and highly revered of the dead. Often the rocks are draped with a white cloth. Someone had tied a red ribbon around the base of the *kakuzotsi fantata* (an act that seemed less exotic when I thought of the Top Ten song of some years back, "Tie a Yellow Ribbon Round the Old Oak Tree").

I asked Maurice if the creek had a name. He said it was called Sahatandra, after the oldest man in the village, who died three years ago. On the way back to the road he found a small boa in the grass, and picked it up and draped it around his neck. It was about three feet long, tan with brown lozenges whose edges caught the sun and by some optical illusion were reproduced as dazzling, blowtorch-blue rings in the air slightly above them. Elsewhere on the island the boa, or *dô*, is thought to be another of the ancestral incarnations and is given a wide berth. Because it often lurks in the cool darkness of family tombs, Malagasies believe the *dô* to be the adult form of the worms that devour the decaying corpses and thus absorb their spirits. But this belief is not found on the eastern escarpment. "Here we believe our ancestors are the indri," Maurice explained.

MOST OF THE people around Perinet belong to a small, politically unimportant ethnic group called the Bezanozano, who are lumbermen and slash-and-burn farmers, clearing the forest and planting dry rice. "Bezanozano means 'inhabitants of the clouds,' right?" I asked Joseph at lunch. That is what Michel, who had taken the train back to Antananarivo, had told me; I was double-checking. "No, it means many small branches," Joseph said. "The people here make fires with many small branches. Other people use regular firewood." Great, I said to myself, beginning to wonder how good the rest of my information was. Joseph called one of the cooks, a native of Perinet and himself a Bezanozano, from the kitchen (both Joseph and Michel were Merina), and the cook backed him up. "What about the name of the creek?" I asked the cook. "Now that the old man it was named for is dead, is the creek going to be renamed? Is it renamed every generation [the way creeks and villages in the hinterland of Zaire are named for the incumbent headman]? Or will it always be Sahatandra?" The cook said that *saha* meant water in the local dialect, while *tandra* was a girl who had drowned in the creek. Her father had lived near a waterfall thirty kilometers away. Maurice, irked at being contradicted, said that *saha* meant a garden plot, a *champs*, not water. The cook said, "No, it means water." "I can't help you with this one," Joseph said. "I know nothing about the origin of the creek's name. The best thing is to go into the village and ask the elders."

So that afternoon Joseph and I crossed the railroad tracks and a footbridge over the river into which the creek emptied (also called the Sahatandra), and, sidestepping rivulets of scum, we climbed a winding muddy path past two-story weathered gray houses with peaked roofs and second-story balconies. The power lines were thatched with spiderwebs to which enormous spiders—the world's second-largest orb-weavers—clung. A bad cold was going around the village; we could hear hacking coughs from within every second house. Joseph said there were seven thousand people in the village, which had been renamed Andasibe, the Big Station in Malagasy, in the early seventies, in the spirit of *authenticité* that was then sweeping many former Francophone colonies. "The people in the forest are poor but happy," he told me. *"Il ne reste que la liberté pour que l'homme soit heureux.* Here in the village there is more misery. There is malaria, and an undescribed mosquito-borne fever called the virus Andasibe, which can be fatal if the person is unhealthy. The humidity takes its toll. I can't sleep because of the aches it brings on in my shoulder when I lie down. But the biggest problem is dehydration from diarrhea, which kills many children." We stopped at the doctor's house—the doctor was Joseph's closest friend, the only person in the village he could talk about the form of life with beside the padre and the two nuns, who were Italian. A woman came to the door and said the doctor couldn't see us because he was laid up with diarrhea. So we continued to the central plaza of the village, where women sat at stalls behind piles of beans, potatos, taro leaves, and a youth was strumming a homemade guitar. On the wall of an alcove in which a man was operating on a radio there was a poster of John Travolta, the mythical American superstar, the universal culture hero of the early eighties, who had been superceded by Michael Jackson (three years ago kids in the Amazon were moonwalking to Jackson's *Thriller* album). Now Jackson was passé: this was the year of Bruce Springsteen, whose posters had just reached Antananarivo. Joseph said that television was due to arrive in Andasibe at the end of the year; the receiving station had already been built on a ridge out of town. I wondered how long it would be before television began to erode the local culture, how soon it would replace gossip and storytelling as the main way of passing the time, as it is doing all over the world, what it would do to these people's hold on their legends and history, which already seemed precarious.

Joseph asked an old man leaning on a balcony above us about the origin of the name Sahatandra and the old man said, "Once there were so many crocodiles in the river that it was *fady* to wash dirty pots or laundry in the river." (These were

Nile crocodiles, *mamba* in Malagasy, which swam over from Africa during the Pleistocene and have been hunted out almost everywhere on the island except in a few lakes in the north, where they are revered as ancestors.) "A woman named Madame Tandra was offered to the crocodiles. After that they disappeared." "When was this?" I asked. "About eighty years ago," the old man said.

Just then the president of the *commune rurale de* Sambademba, the local representative of the *pouvoir révolutionnaire*, came up the path, and Joseph explained to him that we were trying to get to the bottom of the name of the river. He invited us to his office, where his clerk and an old woman in a bandana joined in the discussion. The three of them agreed that according to ancestral beliefs, a woman named Tandra had been sacrificed "more than a hundred years ago to keep the crocodiles from multiplying." It was clear that the dead continued to exert tremendous influence on the villagers' lives. But their reverence for "the ancestors" (*razana*) seemed more ideological than specific. I traced several of their genealogies. None of them could go back more than four generations—typical shallow tropical-forest pedigrees. And yet the woman in the bandana said she had a hundred ancestors in her family tomb, and once a year, she and hundreds of her relatives gathered at the tomb, which was twenty miles from Andasibe, for the *famidahama*, or exhumation ceremony. "Every year we change the shrouds, *nous emballons les restes mortels*," she said. I asked how many of the ancestors she exhumed. "That depends on how much money you have," she said. "The shrouds, the *lambamena*, are very expensive." If you only had money for one, whom would you exhume? "Your mother and father are usually wrapped together," she said. "You would do them first. You would do your grandfather before your uncle or brother." Did she know the names of all the ancestors in the tomb? No. (When we got home, I contacted the anthropologist Robert Dewar, who works on

Madagascar, and he explained that as the disintegration of the older ancestors progresses, their bones are heaped together, and it is impossible to tell them apart. "Every Malagasy," he said, "theoretically has the right to be buried in any of the tombs of his eight great-grandparents, but in reality he usually only has a choice of three. To be buried in a tomb you have to have contributed to its upkeep. It could be on your mother's or your father's side. Or, if you marry a woman who is close to her mother's people, you could end up in their tomb. But if you couldn't stand your in-laws that of course wouldn't happen. Basically it all depends on what part of the family you want to deal with.")

We met Jaosolo at the post office and he said we hadn't got the story about the river's name right at all. There had *never* been crocodiles in the river, he assured us. This had simply been a case of a first wife killing the second while the husband was away, and dumping the body into the river. "*Tandra* means beauty spot," he said. "The second wife had a beauty spot. *Saha* is definitely not a field, it is a brook." But while there were no crocodiles in the river, there were definitely, Jaosolo couldn't resist adding, *zazavavindrano*, mermaids, *sirènes*. "In December they take handsome men and suck their blood, and their cold white bodies float to the surface." (I have heard very similar stories in Zaire and Amazonia.) "Once an old woman was stolen by the *zazavavindrano*," he went on. "They needed a midwife. She was returned a month later unharmed, and the *zazavavindrano* gave her two cows. This is a true story. It happened in 1948 in Maranara, which is a little further downriver and to the north. And during the construction of the railroad the *zazavavindrano* who live under the big falls at Ikuna stole an engineer, a surveyor, and eight bearers to live with them. Every December twenty-fifth offerings are left at the falls." I wondered if they were meant as Christmas presents.

When Joseph and I returned to the hotel, we spoke with

an old Bezanozano waiter, who said "Jaosolo doesn't know anything. He only came here in 'fifty-seven. There used to be many crocodiles. Every time a cow crossed the river it was eaten. One night the parents of Tandra, a rich family with many zebu, dreamed that the genies of the water wanted the girl. These were not the *zazavavindrano*, but the *razana*, the spirits of the ancestors in the water—they wanted her." During the visit to the office of the *président de la commune rurale* I had asked the old woman in the bandana what would happen if you did nothing for your ancestors, and she had said, "They come in your sleep and say 'I'm cold. I need beef.' Or they make you sick. You go to the sorcerer and they speak through him—'you didn't exhume me'—and he directs their appeasement." Sometimes, as in the case of Tandra's parents, the amends you had to make to them were frightening.

The next morning, our last sortie with Maurice, we went to the far end of the reserve, hoping to see some of the eight other species of lemur at Perinet. Very soon, we did—two eastern gentle lemurs—gray, catsized, with long, curly tails, sitting on their haunches at the edge of a bamboo grove, munching young shoots. They saw us and bounded into the darkness of the grove. We could hear the stutter of axes and the steady tear of a saw not far ahead. Soon we came upon seven woodmen. Two of them were up on a makeshift scaffold sawing the trunk of a *ravensara* tree into beams and boards with an eight-foot-long crosscut saw for a Monsieur Georges of Tamatava, a big city on the coast. Monsieur Georges had a logging permit from Eaux et Forêts, which permitted him to choose from forty commercial species. Each of the woodmen received two boxes of rice and less than two dollars a day. They slept in a little hut of pandanus leaves; the pandanus, an agavelike plant, sprouted here and there on the forest floor. "Seen any lemurs?" I asked. "Yes. The brown one," one of them said. "Do you hunt them?" "No, but only because I don't have a gun."

A mile further along, we came on a lemur trap, right on the path. It was for the black and white ruffed lemur, Maurice said. He showed us how it worked: in comes the lemur, enticed by the fruit of a melastome; he trips the wire, and down comes the door—it's as simple as that. The cage was made of stakes planted in the ground and lashed with bark cord. "The penalty for poaching is five years in the prison at Moramanga, but there are only two guards for the reserve. *C'est ça le problème Malgache*," Maurice said sadly. "Almost everybody in the forest poaches, because they have no money to buy meat in the market. They either eat the lemurs or sell them to the Chinese who are working on the Nouvelle Route Nationale Numéro Deux or to *les riches*. That's why it's hard to see the other species." The *président de la commune rurale*, he said, was a known lemur eater. He tore the trap from the ground and flung it into the bush.

Half a mile later we reached the camp of some other woodmen who Maurice suspected had made the trap. Half a dozen men were sitting under a thatch roof on poles, and one was pounding a red-hot hammer into shape on an anvil. "It might be interesting for you to talk to them," Maurice said. I asked if they had seen any lemurs. "None right here, but far away there are some still," one of them answered. ("*C'est ça le problème, monsieur*," Maurice said in an aside while translating.) Which kind? *Babakoto*, *simpoona* (the diademed sifaka), *titi* (the sportive lemur), *kootika* (the gentle), *varika* (the brown), *antigi* (the mouse lemur), *ataca* (the eastern woolly lemur). Do you eat them all? Yes. Even the indri? Yes. "They know indri is an ancestor but they eat him anyway," Maurice explained. "Why? Isn't it *fady*?" I asked. "*Autrefois c'était très fady*," the spokesman of the woodmen went on. "As *fady* as marrying your sister." "So why do you eat it?" I repeated. "Because they are fat and because today there is a *manque de protéine*. We have to eat. A kilo of beef costs a thousand francs in the market at

Andasibe. A lemur may weigh eight kilos, and we can sell it for fifteen hundred francs a kilo." Don't you get punished with sickness for violating the *fady*? "Others get sick, even die, because of their belief," the spokesman said. "These men don't have the belief deeply," Maurice explained. "How do you kill them?" I asked. "With a *flèche*," the spokesman said. I thought this meant an arrow shot from a bow, but when I asked to see a *flèche*, one of them showed me a slingshot with a thong cut from an inner tube, picked up a pebble from the ground and fired it through a nearby banana leaf.

Five hundred yards later we came out on the Nouvelle Route Nationale Numéro Deux. "This is the end of the reserve," Maurice told me. Across the road a charred, burned-out wasteland, acres and acres of smouldering devastation, spread as far as the eye could see. "That is the country of the Betsimasaraka," Maurice told me. The Betsimasaraka are the second-largest ethnic group on the island. They occupy a four-hundred-mile strip of the eastern coast that extends inland twenty to fifty miles, and grow spices—vanilla, cloves—and coffee.

We bought coffee and roasted sweet potatoes that a Betsimasaraka woman was selling in a little hut along the road and sat on the curb eating and drinking. A baby was crying in another hut (Nicky asked, "Here do you have to pay to get babies out of your stomach?") and in the distance some indri were wailing. Their cries seemed even sadder now that I realized how threatened the animals are. These were the cries of the last indri.

A bearded man in a brimless straw hat came from one of the huts and sat on the curb beside us. "Why don't you ask him some questions?" Maurice said. I was tired of asking questions, I just wanted to hang out, but after a while, picked up by the coffee, I asked Maurice to ask the bearded man why it was *fady* to eat the indri (he didn't speak French). Maurice translated his answer: "*Autrefois*, some Bezanozano went into the forest to get some honey. They climbed a vine high into the treetops, but then the vine broke and there was no way back down. The indri came and took them down on their backs. Since then the Bezanozano tell their children, if you eat the indri all the Bezanozano will die." Attenborough had picked up a variant of this story: the men were up in a tree, gathering honey, when they were attacked by bees; they fell and were caught in midair by the indri; and that was the beginning of the friendship.

"What about the *aye-aye?*" I asked. The *aye-aye* is the rarest, and weirdest, of the lemurs, indeed one of the rarest, weirdest animals in the world. It is small, solitary, nocturnal, ghoulish in appearance, with bat ears, bug eyes, and a long, thin, fleshless third finger with which it taps trees to see if they are hollow and extracts insects from decaying wood. Its contact call is *cree*; its alarm cry is *rontsit*. Until a few years ago there were thought to be only fifty *aye-aye* left, but there are indications that they may be more numerous. Two holes thought to have been gnawed by an *aye-aye* had recently been found in a tree on the reserve.

"The *aye-aye,*" the bearded man said, "is a kind of man. He has different kinds of hair: human, dog's, chicken's, pig's, cow's. He is like a god. He has much power. Some people here find an *aye-aye* and kill him with a stick, then they go down the road a few yards, and the *aye-aye* comes back to life and follows them." A Peugeot wagon headed for Brickaville, crammed full of people and baskets, with TAXI KOFOTO painted on its door, whizzed by five feet in front of us.

"If the sorcerer of the attackers is not strong," the bearded man continued, "the *aye-aye* and his attackers change places: the attackers die, and the *aye-aye* lives." (The word he used for sorcerer was marvelous: *mpanaofanafody.*) "When you hunt the *aye-aye* or immediately afterwards, to avoid its power, crush a tobacco leaf and rub the juice on your face," he advised.

"There are still many *aye-aye*," he said. "You find their nests in the cutover scrub." Can you show us one? I asked. "Without a sorcerer it is taboo to look at one," he said. "Can you take us to a sorcerer?" "That can be arranged," he said with a little smile. "Well, then, come on—let's go," I said, getting up excitedly. Both he and Maurice were smiling now, enjoying a little joke. "He is the sorcerer," Maurice finally explained.

The next communication from the bearded man came as no surprise. "He needs a hundred and fifty francs for *tafy*, medicine," Maurice translated. "The *aye-aye* is the enemy of the sorcerer." I handed him the money. We went into a tiny hut, eight by eight, with a ceiling so low I couldn't stand up in it. A woman—the sorcerer's wife—vacated the room, and the sorcerer took down a modern medicine canister from a shelf. The canister was labeled POLYVINYLPYRROLIDONE, twenty pills. "What's that for?" I asked. "He doesn't know, he found it on the road," Maurice relayed. The sorcerer opened the canister and poured out a few dozen hard black *famelura* beans and picking up a handful, scattered it on the table we had crowded around. Then he sorted the beans into two vertical rows, in groups of 2, 2, 1, 1, 2, 1, 2 and 2, 2, 1, 1, 2, 1, 1. Then he asked my name. I gave it. He added two beans to the last group in the first row, and two to the last group in the second row, and pondered the result. At last he announced: "We will see the nest but not the animal." "Why?" I asked. "Because he left during the night and is now far away." "What is the nest like?" I asked. "Like a bird's but very big, with many branches in the form of a bed." "How did he find the nest?" "The beans have told me where it is, and now I will tell you," the sorcerer said. "I have never seen it before myself." Where is it? "Near." We went into the next hut, a store, where he bought some tobacco. "I need rum, for the prayer," he said through Maurice. Another three hundred francs.

Then he led us down the road. I asked Maurice if he thought the sorcerer was doing a number on us. *"C'est un sorcier pour faire le mauvais, pas pour faire le vrai,"* he told me. "There are better sorcerers on the coast." After half a mile the bearded man took a faint path that led up a steep slope to a tree. Fifteen feet up the tree there was a tangle of vines with a mess of leaves in it. He thrust a pole up at it. "That's it," he said. "That's it?" I asked. It looked dubious. Leaves would have got caught among the vines of themselves, without help from an animal. The sorcerer uncorked the rum and sprinkled some on the base of the tree, then he steeled himself with a healthy swig and, trembling with fear, with tears of fright forming in his eyes, he looked up at the nest and prayed for the *aye-aye* and for our health. "He was very sincere," I said to Maurice after we had left him and doubled back into the reserve. "He believed." And who was I to question the power of belief?

THE EMPEROR
WHO ATE HIS
PEOPLE

Between sessions of the trial of the ex-emperor Jean-Bédel
Bokassa in Bangui, I sometimes sat on the balcony of my room
on the eighth floor of the Hotel Sofitel (the Safari in Bokassa's
day), trying to make sense of the complicated, grisly story that
was unfolding at the Palais de Justice. According to the in-
dictment against him, Bokassa had eaten people (the charge
was "anthropophagy" and procuring cadavers for the purpose of
anthropophagy), clubbed schoolchildren to death, poisoned his
two-day-old grandson, assassinated dozens of his advisers. The
catalogue of his atrocities went on and on. He was, along with
Idi Amin Dada of Uganda and Masie Nguema Biyogo of Equatorial Guinea, one of the three *grands monstres* of postcolonial
Africa.

In 1966, six years after the Central African Republic became an independent state, Bokassa—with the support of the
French—took over as president. In 1977 he declared himself
emperor, and spent $25 million on a bizarrely lavish coronation.
Two years later, when his outrages became embarrassing for
Giscard d'Estaing, the French had him deposed in a coup that
reinstated the man he had kicked out originally. He spent four
years in exile in the Ivory Coast, and three years in a run-down
château outside Paris. Now he was back, of his own volition,

mysteriously, and standing trial for a multitude of crimes, many of which he had already been convicted of *in absentia*. The most puzzling question was how such an obvious psychotic could have stayed in power for so long.

Here at the Sofitel, a luxurious air-conditioned high rise perched right on the Ubangi River and sealed off from the suffering of the country, it was hard to imagine that such horrible things had ever happened. I could have sat on my balcony forever, watching lesser-striped swallows and overwintering European house martins swoop gracefully below, a pied crow hassling a black kite, and beyond them the pageant of the river: fifty-foot dugouts laden with palm oil and manioc roots, scattered over the glassy water like milling fish; fishermen casting nets from exposed rocks along which it was now almost possible to walk all the way across the river to Zaire. The river was so low it had been unnavigable for several months, and the hydroelectricity it generated for the city was unpredictable. There were frequent *pannes d'électricité*, both sudden blackouts and sequential ones, as the juice was turned off in one *quartier* and on in another as a conservation measure. Beyond the fishermen, I could see the first few miles of the Ubangi's twisting descent to the Zaire river, hundreds of miles away, and, in the far distance, the gigantic, close-packed trees of the world's second-largest rain forest, Conrad's heart of darkness, Stanley's darkest Africa. Bangui is on the northern edge of it.

BELOW THE BALCONY I sometimes saw François Gibault, one of Bokassa's French lawyers—a specialist in sensational political trials—floating in the pool in the lotus position, unwinding after his profitable day's work. A group of expatriates were usually drinking in the wicker chairs nearby—safari-jacketed types like General Shmuel Gonen, the Israeli hero of the Six-

Day War, now retired, who came to the C.A.R. to be Bokassa's diamond consultant and has been in business for himself since the coup that sent Bokassa into exile. "Nothing has changed," he told me. "There are some things here that we will never understand." Bokassa's yacht used to lie at anchor right below the hotel, and the riverbank was lined with boats; now there were only half a dozen dugouts. Such scenes make some people nostalgic for Bokassa's short-lived empire of the late seventies, when everybody had work and there was a lot of money changing hands and the country counted for something; now the country is broke and everyone is terrified of AIDS.

A knock at the door. I let in a young man who says he has come to turn down my bed. He turns down my bed—a simple operation, but he isn't satisfied with it. He untucks it and turns it down again, then goes over to the other side and sees how it looks from there. Occasionally he looks up at me. I know what is happening: he wants to be my friend. Whatever I'm after here, he's my man. What's your name? I ask. Philippe. He wants to be an English professor, he tells me, although he doesn't know English yet. Married? No. Any kids? One. The mother lives with her parents, *comme je ne suis pas encore très bien assis.* You free tomorrow? I ask him. I need to go to Kolongo. Will you take me there? *"Pas problème."*

THE NEXT MORNING—Sunday morning—Philippe came for me in a cab and we drove along the quay, between rows of ancient trees dripping with ripe mangoes, which people were knocking down with long bamboo poles. We passed the Rock Hotel and a stark-naked, dust-covered young man scavenging in a ditch —an *aliéné*, Philippe explained, a crazy, the Central African equivalent of a bag lady; *il s'en fout.* Then we continued past the heavily guarded radio station, the first place insurgents head for when there has been a coup, to broadcast that they've taken over. Soon we had left the *centre ville* and were driving along the river, past the slaughterhouse where several hundred zebu cattle were waiting in pens, and before long we arrived at a derelict pastel-pink-walled compound with a sign saying "Kolongo Extension of the University of Bangui." The gate was chained. We called for the guard and he came and let us in. I said I was covering the *procès Bokassa* and wondered if he could show me around. *Pas problème.*

Kolongo began as a villa built by Bokassa between 1974 and 1976 to house La Roumaine, the strapping blond Rumanian cabaret singer he took a fancy to and married. Bokassa had several official wives and even more mistresses, whom he kept under guard, in virtual imprisonment, in separate villas. The most important wives were La Roumaine and Catherine, a sensational Central African beauty who had been a stewardess. One of her former colleagues at Air Zaire told me he wasn't sure how they'd met, but he recalled a flight he piloted that she wasn't on in which Bokassa, his entourage, and the stewardesses became involved in an orgy. Catherine became his empress, and La Roumaine, his number-two wife, settled in at Kolongo, which Bokassa expanded into his in-town palace. The place was now in ruins. Ten-foot weeds, two-foot termite bells, several species of chameleon scuttling around, freezing, swiveling one eye, doing nervous push-ups, fantastic butterflies catching the sun, the bulletproof windows knocked out, complicated division problems and graffiti scrawled over the walls—it was a beautiful example of the rapidity of tropical decay.

The guard and a young economics student took us over to the place where Bokassa had held kangaroo court, sitting under a canopy. His ministers sat over there, on the right, the prisoner stood there, in the middle of those flagstones—they acted it all out: "O.K., what do you have to say for yourself?" and if he doesn't think you're telling the truth he beckons to his soldiers and they feed you to the lions or the crocodiles, depending on his mood. We went into the lions' cage, in a bunker with huge baobabs sprouting from it, and on to a passage in back where the condemned man was handcuffed.

What kind of people did the lions eat? *Hauts placés*, political biggies, the economics student told me, except for the lion keeper, who was caught stealing meat from the lions to feed his family. But the lions wouldn't eat him, and the next day he was transferred to the crocodiles. We went over to the crocodile pool, which was empty. Bokassa claimed at his trial that the crocodiles were "simply for decoration," but the French soldiers who broke into Kolongo on the day of the coup dredged the pool and found the gnawed remains of several human skeletons. A Central African journalist I had dinner with one night told me with tears running down her face that Bokassa had a supernatural power that made people tremble and obey him, and that he got this power from the animals—the lions, crocodiles, and snakes he raised. "If he saw you were strong he said, Let's see how you make out against my animals, and laughed. He did this for fourteen years. It's not normal."

The villa itself is in back, past a game park where gazelles and antelopes had grazed in the shade of *kolongo* trees, which are a kind of fan palm. It consists of dozens of small rooms, now gutted, looking on a series of courtyards, most of which were never used but which Bokassa could keep an eye on with a closed-circuit surveillance system in his bedroom. Most of the rooms were arranged around several interior courtyards with pillars of carved jutting-breasted African caryatids, one on top of the other, holding up the terrace roofs. *"C'était beau. Mais c'est disparu,"* the economics student declared with a dramatic sweep of his hands and a crazed look on his face. *"Les hautes qualités restaient ici."* We looked into the snake room—Bokassa raised cobras, vipers, and a *très vénéneux* khaki-colored type called a *ngbo*. A huge bumblebee, the size of a hummingbird,

buzzed by. I started to copy the graffiti in my notebook—
they comprised a people's verdict. BOKOSSA [sic] HOMME
DUR DE LA R.C.A., one said. IL N'EST PAS À OUBLIER, said
another.

"This was La Roumaine's bedroom," the guardian told me,
gesturing at the ruined wreck of her revolving bed. Sometimes
Bokassa would not show up for weeks, and La Roumaine would
manage to get someone to drive her to Berengo, where she would
throw a hysterical scene in front of everybody, calling him an
ugly monkey. Her baby's nanny informed Bokassa that she had
once, in a desperate attempt to alleviate her boredom, borrowed
the cook's velocipede and taken it for a ride outside the compound, which was a no-no. The cook was killed by pepper,
which was put in his eyes, nose, ears, and elsewhere. Then one
of La Roumaine's maids, pretty Adele Mokossian-tendele, out
of jealousy, informed Bokassa that La Roumaine was getting it
on with the security guards, and that one of the other maids,
Martine N'Doute, was involved in these orgies. So one night
Bokassa sneaked up to Kolongo on foot and surprised La Roumaine with one of the guards. The guard slipped on his shorts
and jumped into the pool (now a quarter full of scummy green
water, the walls cracked, a dozen frogs floating in it). Bokassa
had the police search Martine's belongings and among them they
found an *album d'amour*, full of explicit pictures of her and La
Roumaine with four of the guards. Three of the guards were
killed in Ngaragba. The fourth, Tita Sambasola, survived and
was freed after the coup, and he testified at the trial. Bokassa's
defense: I couldn't tolerate such conduct between my wife, my
maid, and the security guards, which is why I had them arrested
and ordered to be killed. But he spared his wife. La Roumaine
was allowed to leave the country. Her present whereabouts are
unknown. Graffiti on wall of their bedroom: BOKASSA C'EST MOI
QUI BAISE CATHERINE ET LA GABRIELLE EN FRANCE. On a wall
outside an enigmatic poem:

PETIT À PETIT
L'OISEAU FAIT SON NID
MAIS VOILÀ BOKASSA
EST DISPARU
NE PRESSE LA VIE

The economics student interprets it for me. It means *va douce-
ment*, go slowly, like the bird who builds his nest little by little.
Don't be too *pressé*, look what happened to Bokassa.

Last stop on the tour, a room the guard calls the abattoir,
the slaughterhouse. See, he said, the bodies were cut into small
pieces on this table, the blood ran out in these troughs in the
floor, then the pieces were kept in these cold-storage rooms. I
looked into the rooms. There was an outer room and an inner
one. In the ceiling of an adjoining room the guard showed me
a cardboard box where he said the French soldiers found the
torso of the mathematics teacher Massangue, which was identified by his relatives.

BOKASSA'S TRIAL WAS held four days a week, from two to seven.
The day after I got back from Kolongo, I took in the fifty-first
session. As I stood in front of the Palais de Justice waiting to
be let in, two soldiers came from another building carrying the
ermine-lined red robes and round red hats with black and yellow
bands of the president of the court, the four *assesseurs*, and the
prosecutor; they walked past another couple of dozen soldiers
lounging around in the nearly hundred-degree heat and went
through the front door. Nobody had bothered to raise the tattered
flag of the Central African Republic over the door. It lay wilted
at the base of its pole.

Maybe fifteen minutes later—it was so hot everything seemed
to take ages, to be happening in slow motion—an armored car
pulled up, and out of it came a short, stocky old man in a black

suit, balding, with gray-white hair and a sparse woolly beard—
Bokassa. He didn't look like a monster. Smiling and joking with
the soldiers, he looked like a nice old man, older than his official
age of sixty-six. He was having trouble walking. His lawyers
had moved unsuccessfully for a postponement on the grounds
that he had high blood pressure; they only had won permission
for him to sit during the proceedings. In the beginning he had
had to stand before the president of the court five hours straight.

Inside the courtroom, a windowless auditorium with ventilation chinks in the cinder-block walls, the French lawyers,
Gibault and Francis Szpiner—short, self-confident men in black
robes with white bibs—carried their briefcases to the table
behind Bokassa's chair. Szpiner is flamboyant, a veteran of
scandalous corruption cases. Gibault is more refined and me-
thodical. He successfully defended the Moroccan minister of
the interior who was accused of kidnapping and killing an opposition leader in Paris in 1965. Another French lawyer, Ber-
nard Jouanneau, who has been hired by the C.A.R. to get back
the money Bokassa stole, and his property abroad, sat on the
prosecution side. This week the prosecution was concentrating
on the *détournements*—how Bokassa during his last two years
in power diverted 17 million Central African francs (to convert
into dollars, divide by 265) a week from the national treasury
into a secret fund which he used to buy—in France alone—
three châteaux, a hotel, a farm, and a villa, Le Patio, in Nice.
He took the money out in military strongboxes each time he
went out of the country.

I went up to the gallery, and sat with several Central Africans who were filming the proceedings for a telecast that night
to the five thousand or so *privilégiés* who have TV sets. It was
sweltering. Everybody was fanning himself rapidly, and my shirt
was soon soaked. The scene below, illuminated by TV flood-
lights, was like a tropical Daumier. The prosecutor, Gabriel-

Faustin M'Bodou, stood in his ermine robe at a raised desk to the left, and the president, Édouard Franck, flanked by the *assesseurs*, sat at a long, raised table in the middle, under a plaque representing the scales of justice, with a legend above, in Sangho, the national language, *Zo Kwe Zo* (all people are equal), and below, *So Zo La* (all people are to be respected). M'Bodou explained to the court how Bokassa got the money out of the treasury. His oratorical style was rapid-fire and inspired, like a revivalist preacher or a headman addressing his people in the village plaza. At one point Gibault jumped up with an objection. Professing astonishment, he said, "But we are *en plein surréalisme*," and the scene became briefly like a cock-fight, with him and M'Bodou hissing at each other in staccato bursts of polysyllabic French. Then Bokassa got up and gave his version of the story, a long, rambling, impressively detailed self-exculpation. His voice was that of a man convinced of his innocence. You almost believed him, except for his eyes, cunning eyes that kept darting to the side. The proceedings were being broadcast live by Radio Bangui, and the entire country —in bars, guardhouses, taxis, private homes, every dusty little village in the north—was tuned in. That voice, so persuasive and controlling, going on for hours, dominating the airwaves again, must have sent chills down many spines. At one point a few days earlier a spontaneous shout had gone up in the city: He's lying!

During a break in the action, I talked with the man next to me, a journalist for the local TV station, who turned out to be a Bokassa victim himself. Ten years ago, returning from Addis Ababa, Bokassa had summoned the press to tell about his trip. On the radio that night the journalist had described the meeting as *une déclaration*, a statement, rather than *une conférence de presse*, because nobody had asked Bokassa any questions. Bokassa for some reason was offended by this and had the man brought to the palace, where his soldiers beat him to a bloody pulp. Then he was taken to Ngaragba and left there for a year. What was it like? I asked. "*Affreux, dur, inhumain.* We reproach him for reigning so cruelly," he said, "for not having administrative guidelines for punishing small, professional mistakes. A colleague of mine was beaten for announcing the death of Pompidou. *Il ne savait que ça.*"

Then the TV camera broke down and nobody could get it working again, and the trial was over for the day. It was the only functional TV camera in the country.

THE CENTRAL AFRICAN Republic, like so many of the new countries in this part of the world, is not so much a country as it is an anarchic collection of tribes, an invention of the French. Two things, however, have facilitated the lumping together of the C.A.R.'s eighty-odd tribes: they all speak the same language, Sangho, and they share a long history of oppression. All but the Pygmies and several river tribes along the Ubangi were driven into the area by Arab slavers, who continued to raid their villages as late as 1910. By then the French, the Belgians, and the British, who had been fighting over Central Africa, had come to an agreement. The British got the Nile Valley, to the East, the Belgians got most of the Congo Valley, and the French got what became known as French Equatorial Africa, comprising several territories: Gabon, the Middle Congo, Chad, and Ubangi-Shari—the last a well-watered plateau slightly smaller than Texas, bounded by the Ubangi River on the south and drained by the Shari in the north. Bangui was founded in 1889, and it grew quickly into a thriving exploitative center. The region was rich in diamonds, timber, gold, ivory, and docile natives who could be put to work mining, building railroads, growing cotton, gathering rubber. In 1925 André Gide traveled through Ubangi-Shari and described it as "a country in ruins for the profit of a few." Villages and fields were abandoned, malnutrition and starvation were widespread.

One of the many victims of those years was a man named Mgboundoulou, who was caned to death by a French administrator in 1927. Mgboundoulou belonged to the M'Baka, a small tribe in the forest south of Bangui who account for only seven percent of the C.A.R.'s three million-plus people but have contributed an inordinate number of its civil servants. A week after his murder, Mgboundoulou's wife committed suicide from grief, leaving twelve orphans to be brought up by thirty-two uncles. One of the orphans was six-year-old Jean-Bédel, who was called Bokassa because he had been born in a little forest near the Berengo swamp, where years later he would build a palace; *bokassa* means little forest in M'Baka.

Jean-Bédel was educated by Catholic missionaries, but instead of becoming a priest he became a soldier, fighting against the Nazis in the Free French Resistance under De Gaulle, who became one of his heroes (at De Gaulle's funeral in 1970 Bokassa sobbed uncontrollably, "Papa, Papa"), and later serving in the French colonial infantry in Indochina, where he was decorated and commissioned. After World War II, the French rewarded the Central Africans for their assistance by continuing the colonial system, and the Central Africans reacted with anger. In 1955, when a Frenchman who had badly beaten his cook and his cook's wife went unpunished, riots broke out, and for a time there was open war on Europeans. Three years later De Gaulle decided that it was pointless to try to maintain the empire any longer, and the territories of French Equatorial Africa found themselves on their own, countries.

UBANGI-SHARI WAS now the Central African Republic. Its first president, Barthélémy Boganda, was, like Bokassa, a M'Baka who had been orphaned by brutal colonials. But Boganda was a priest turned political activist. Revered by his people, he was not destined to lead them for long. Scarcely had he composed the national anthem and designed the flag when he was killed in a plane crash. He was succeeded by his inept nephew, David Dacko, who presided over increasing turmoil as his people left their villages and fields en masse to look for diamonds, and the economy went to pot. By 1965 the republic was ripe for a coup. After foiling a takeover attempt by the chief of police, Lieutenant Colonel Bokassa, the chief of staff of the armed forces and a cousin of Dacko's, took advantage of the general revelry on New Year's Eve to mount a coup of his own.

Immediately executing his ten most dangerous rivals, abolishing the Constitution of 1959, dissolving the National Assembly, and assuming all legislative and executive powers, the new president embarked on a program of modernization, increasing diamond and uranium production, building roads, a new hospital and slaughterhouse. But within a few years reports of "a disturbing element of personal savagery" began to appear in stories about him by the foreign press. In 1969 he executed a high-ranking Cabinet member for plotting his overthrow, and four years later the minister of public works was taken to Ngaragba for the same reason and was never seen again. Not only were suspected traitors punished harshly, but all of their relatives, who might seek revenge on him, were eliminated. One case was discussed in detail at Bokassa's trial: that of General Martin Linpoupou, who was sentenced to ten years for plotting a coup in 1974; Bokassa had his brothers, cousins, and even his mother killed. His mother allegedly had four (or according to other testimony three) breasts and was therefore considered to be a sorceress who could have effected her son's miraculous escape and had to be liquidated. The court would pay close attention to the testimony about the number of breasts of Linpoupou's mother, because killing a sorceress under Central African law is a much less serious offense than killing an ordinary citizen.

Not all Bokassa's victims were political. Beggars with shriveled limbs and other birth defects, who he felt were a shame to the race, were periodically taken off the streets of Bangui, flown up in planes, and dropped into the river. When some of the cows on his farm at Berengo died, Sangou Bessanque, the veterinarian, was taken away and killed. The schoolteacher Zanga Archile was sentenced to ten years by a military court for giving subversive instruction, but was killed in prison on Bokassa's orders. Bokassa's defense for the last two: "I regret to hear these people were killed. It was done without my knowledge. If I had known I would not have authorized it."

Bokassa was particularly hard on thieves. In 1971 he decreed that thieves caught for the first time would have their left ears cut off (the term for this punishment was *ablation*), second-time offenders would lose their right ears, third-time offenders a hand, and the fourth time they would be hanged. That year Bokassa celebrated Mother's Day by having everyone in prison for a crime against a woman hanged at dawn. In 1972, furious that his war on crime seemed to be having little effect, he invited foreign photographers to watch his soldiers club and kick forty or so petty thieves, after which they were left in the sun and several died.

Bokassa's erratic behavior didn't always have hideous consequences, as in the strange case of the two Martines, which seemed to reveal a benevolent side to his character. In 1970 he made an all-out effort to find a daughter he had fathered in Vietnam; he knew only that her name was Martine and that she would now be seventeen. There was no shortage of seventeen-year-old half-Vietnamese Martines in Vietnam, because in 1953 the French movie actress Martine Carol was at the height of her stardom, and many of the French soldiers stationed there that year named their children with local women after her. Finally, in November, Bokassa announced his choice from a stack of photographs forwarded by the French Embassy in Saigon, and the girl, who had been found selling cigarettes in one of the city's slums, was flown to Bangui, where Bokassa, with tears streaming down his cheeks, gave her a full state welcome at the airport and took her into his already enormous family (there are more than fifty recognized offspring).

But this was not the real Martine. A month later a second Martine surfaced, with the right identification and the right scar, and she was given the same elaborate, lachrymose airport welcome. The other Martine was allowed to remain in the family. Both made good marriages: the real Martine to a doctor, the false Martine to a young army officer, Fidel Obrou, who became the commander of the presidential guard. But this story, too, had a terrible ending.

On February 3, 1976, Obrou tried to blow up Bokassa with a hand grenade, but missed. He and ten other conspirators were promptly taken before a firing squad. The next day his widow, who was in advanced pregnancy, entered the hospital and was put up in the presidential suite, where the real Martine's husband delivered her son. Several days later the baby died under mysterious circumstances, perhaps from poison administered by the doctor under Bokassa's orders. Poisoning the baby was one of the fourteen charges against Bokassa when he returned from exile two years ago. A nurse testified that the false Martine had told her that Bokassa had said the baby would have to be killed if it turned out to be a boy. When the nurse stepped down from the witness chair, Bokassa, instead of responding with one of his customary lengthy refutations, remained in his seat and stayed silent, visibly shaken. The current whereabouts of the two Martines are unknown.

THERE ARE SEVERAL theories about how Bokassa became such a monster. Some claim that he was crazy from the beginning, permanently deranged by the loss of his parents. As an adult, perhaps acting under a repetition compulsion, he would kill half a dozen children in exactly the way his father was murdered, by caning them to death. Others argue that he became a monster only after he took power, that a certain percentage of people who find themselves with unlimited means at their disposal and no constraints on their behavior will become monsters, and that he was one of them. Still others believe that he shows the childlike, paranoiac comportment and the inability to stick to one train of thought typical of someone in the tertiary stage of syphilis, which he could have picked up in Indochina, and that if he had not been able to compensate for the problem with tremendous native cunning, he would never have lasted so long in power. Others say it was drink: he knocked off about a fifth of Chivas Regal a day; somebody was always standing by, waiting to refill his glass. Others say that he was simply an anachronism, that in many ways he acted just like a traditional tribal chief, who must deal quickly and decisively with his enemies and keep his people in a state of constant fear or they will not respect him; that Africans expect a certain amount of arbitrary cruelty from their leaders. To this day his rating with many of the members of his tribe is high. But an official in the current government to whom I spoke didn't buy this theory. "Bokassa was not a *vrai chef*," he told me. "He was following an individual psychological trajectory, the personal itinerary of a dictator. A real chief has charisma and he respects his people. He has *la vraie force*. Those without *la vraie force* are obliged to be brutal."

Of course, the more carefully one investigates the anatomy of a monster, the clearer it becomes that he, the *grand monstre*, is only the head, that the rest of the body is composed of *petits monstres* and *tout-petits monstres* who are going along for the ride; of informants who are willing to denounce fellow citizens in the hope of being rewarded with a car, a hotel to manage, a diplomatic post abroad; and of a cowed general population without whose acquiescence none of his monstrosities would be possible. Two of Bokassa's main *petits monstres* were Joseph Mokwa, a commandant of Ngaragba, who was executed in 1980 for his role in a massacre of schoolchildren, and a Pole named Otto Sacher, who was in charge of feeding the prisoners, or, more often than not, of denying them food—one of those gleeful Holocaust types—who skipped the country when the trouble started and whose current whereabouts are also unknown. Most of the killings were carried out in the central prison, under the supervision of Mokwa. It was he who cut off the penis of General Jean-Claude Mandaba and delivered it, as requested, to Bokassa. Mandaba belonged to Fidel Obrou's tribe. After Obrou's failed assassination attempt, Bokassa recalled him from Romania, where he was serving as ambassador, and he was arrested as he stepped off the plane.

Bokassa's excesses were not only sadistic. His greed was boundless. He cornered monopolies on his country's diamonds, ivory, coffee, even insecticides. With funds from the national treasury he made his village bloom, and set up the largest industrial complex in the country at his Berengo palace, where government employees turned out furniture, buttons, records, bricks, and school uniforms, which he sold tax free to the state. Perhaps his most devious scam involved the DC-4 De Gaulle gave him as a present, which he then sold to Air Afrique. After Air Afrique had fixed it up, he had it seized when it landed in Bangui, and then he rented it to the state for his own use on official trips.

He also seems to have been a sex maniac. This, too, was part of the image of the potent chief, to have any woman he wanted, to be like Mobutu in Zaire, the last part of whose full name, Mobutu Sese Seko Kuku Ngbendu Waza Banga, means "the cock who jumps on anything that moves." There were eight love nests on the first floor of Bokassa's palace at Berengo, and a bevy of black and white secretaries, a *régiment féminin*, and a studio of seamstresses from whom he could choose. His chief of protocol's main job was to bring him women; sometimes when he spotted a beauty in the crowd he would stop an official procession and say, Bring her to me tonight. Often he would cruise the *quartiers populaires* of Bangui himself with a suitcase full of bank notes, looking for women. He had a special weakness for twelve-year-olds (the nymphet's parents would get a couple of thousand dollars, a velocipede, or maybe even a house for letting him have his way with her) and for blondes.

BEFORE I GOT to the Central African Republic, I was pretty sure that the stories about Bokassa eating people would turn out to be a case of what could be called figurative cannibalism. Many rural Zaïrois, for instance, believe that Europeans are cannibals. The belief stems in part from the fact that Zaïrois sometimes had their hands cut off by the Belgians if they hadn't collected their daily rubber quota, and in part from a confusion about Holy Communion: anybody who eats the body and drinks the blood of his god, they reasoned, must be a cannibal. In 1981 I walked into a BaLese village deep in the Ituri Forest of northeastern Zaire, and everybody bolted because they thought I had come to eat them. The Zaïrois belief that Europeans are cannibals is a metaphor of oppression, as I thought Bokassa's cannibalism would prove to be. But the more I looked into it the more convinced I became that he actually *did* eat people.

There are many kinds of cannibalism. Revenge cannibalism—the gloating, triumphant ingestion of a slain enemy's heart, liver, or other vital parts—is common at the warring-chiefdom stage of social evolution. Emergency cannibalism was resorted to by the Uruguayan soccer team whose plane crashed in the

Andes. Ritual endocannibalism is practiced by certain tribes like the Yanonamo of northern Amazonia, whose women drink the pulverized ashes of slain kin mixed with banana gruel before their men go off on a raiding party. In the Kindu region of Zaire there are to this day leopard men who wear leopard skins, smear their bodies with leopard grease (which protects them even from lions), chip their teeth to points, and attack and eat people. Among their victims were some Italian soldiers who were part of the U.N. peace-keeping force during the turbulence after independence in 1960. The rarest kind of cannibals are gustatory cannibals—people who are actually partial to the taste of human flesh.

In the last six months there have been two reported instances of cannibalism in Bangui. Several people were caught trying to pass off dried human flesh as beef in the market of one of the *quartiers populaires*, and five *bandits méchants*, who lived in the forest in the *quartier* of Combatant, near the airport, confessed to having mugged and eaten seven people; they were denounced by a boy whom they had sent into town to buy some manioc to eat with their latest victim. The Central African term for such cannibals is *carnivores*.

No Central African whom I asked was particularly surprised that Bokassa should have been a cannibal; the idea of eating human flesh is not as strange and repellent in Africa as it is in Europe. Idi Amin was overthrown the same year as Bokassa, and it emerged that he too was into cannibalism, and that he had boasted that he derived his power from eating people. When I asked why Bokassa had eaten people, Central Africans invariably said, as the guard at Kolongo did, *"pour renforcer son pouvoir."* So this seems to be a case of revenge cannibalism—state-level revenge cannibalism, wherein a chief of *state* ate the hearts, livers, etc. of his enemies so that their power would pass over into him. But perhaps there was also an element of gustatory cannibalism.

Bokassa's tribe, the M'Baka, has a reputation for eating people. A man who had served time in Ngaragba told me that he had learned there that the M'Baka have a special chant they break into when they are partaking of human flesh. (It goes something like "M'baka o, o, o. . . .") When I drove down into the country of the M'Baka, my driver, who was from a different tribe, said, "Everybody here eats people, *entre eux*. If I went into the bush, they would kill me, and my parts would be distributed to their families. But it's a very secret affair, as private as your sexual habits or *gris-gris* [fetishes]—not anything you're going to get them to talk about."

A check of the ethnographic literature seems to bear out these stories. In a 1910 monograph called *Notes Ethnographiques sur les Populations M'Baka*, a certain Dr. Poutrin reports that the M'Baka were cannibals. (One wonders how much of this extraordinary document is to be believed—the evident relish with which Poutrin falls on his subject makes one suspicious— but my experience with early ethnographic material is that it usually has a basis of truth.) According to Poutrin, the M'Baka were well built, robust, and wild, and in their custom and way of life most like the Fans and the Niam-Niam, who were also cannibals. War or battles often broke out among the M'Baka and their neighbors for petty reasons, and the battles were often violent. Victims were heartlessly killed and the dead and wounded enemies were eaten by the victorious tribe. Dr. Poutrin attributes this custom to the scarcity of other meat, concluding (he was probably wrong on this, unaware of the reasoning behind revenge cannibalism) that it was a matter of necessity rather than a savage cult or a morbid ritual. Human flesh, he goes on, was considered a true feast. After a battle, wounded or dead enemies were brought into the village and were tied to a pole. The chief, who always had first choice, circled with red paint the parts he wanted and the warriors chose their morsels; then the corpses were cut up and distributed and eaten on the spot. The buttocks, upper thighs, upper arms, heart, liver, brain, breasts, and female genitals were considered the tastiest pieces. Even in time of peace, when there were no dead enemies, the M'Baka fattened up young girls or bought them from other tribes and ate them. But despite (or why not because of?) their barbaric eating habits, Poutrin concludes, the M'Baka were considered more courageous, cunning, intelligent, and physically stronger than other, noncannibalistic tribes.

PROVING THAT BOKASSA himself ate people is a difficult matter; the evidence has long been digested. The prosecution's case rested on two important witnesses. One was Bokassa's cook, Philippe Linguissa, who testified that he and Bokassa together took flesh out of the cold-storage rooms at Kolongo and that Bokassa asked him to cook a meal, "which I did and he ate it in my presence and seemed to appreciate it." Seventy-five-year-old Linguissa lost a little credibility when he said that while feeding the body into a meat grinder one of the hands detached and gripped him. When the court expressed doubt, he said angrily, "I am not a child. I know what I'm saying. If I'm lying, Mr. President, I'm prepared for the court to have me killed." Bokassa got up and said he'd never seen the man.

The other witness was David Dacko, Bokassa's cousin and president of the Central African Republic both immediately before and after Bokassa's tenure, who said he was shown pictures of cut-up bodies found in the freezer at Kolongo the day after the coup. A reporter who was in Bangui told me that the pieces were trussed up with string like rib roasts and that they were positively identified as human flesh by the coroner. He himself went into the cold-storage rooms, which reeked of the unmistakable sickly sweet smell of human flesh. Anyone who has been in a war would recognize it immediately, he told me. There is nothing quite like it.

For some reason the coroner was not called as a prosecution witness at the trial, nor was his report introduced as evidence. Bokassa's lawyers were confident he would beat the cannibalism charge through lack of evidence. Not that it was a grave one anyway, because under Central African law anthropophagy is only a misdemeanor, and in 1981 the new president of the C.A.R. declared amnesty for all misdemeanors committed prior to his taking office, so even if Bokassa were convicted of eating people, he couldn't be punished for it.

ALTHOUGH IT SEEMS unbelievable that Bokassa could have stayed in power for as long as he did, there was a side to him, obscured now by the gruesome revelations of his cruelty, that appealed to Westerners. I was told that he could be impishly charming at dinner parties in Paris, dispensing diamonds to other guests. He was a shrewd international strategist who attracted twenty-eight embassies and the headquarters of two regional African organizations to Bangui. He put a two-hundred-thousand-acre hunting preserve in the northeastern corner of the country at the disposal of French president Giscard d'Estaing, and beginning in 1974 Giscard came at least once a year to shoot elephants (and, according to Bokassa, to dally with the local women). Giscard attended banquets at Kolongo, little suspecting that—or so Bokassa would later tell one of his lawyers—the delicious entrecôtes were human flesh.

It wasn't until Bokassa beat up on a white journalist that the West became really indignant. The victim was a correspondent for the Associated Press named Michael Goldsmith. On July 14, 1977, Goldsmith was telexing a routine story from Bangui to the A.P. bureau in Johannesburg when there was a brief *panne d'électricité*, causing several lines of gibberish to be printed with the story. These were shown to the chief of police, who decided that they must be some kind of code and that

Goldsmith was a spy for South Africa. Later that day Goldsmith was arrested and driven out to Berengo and taken before Bokassa, who without a word of explanation laid open Goldsmith's forehead with the heavy ivory-inlaid ebony cane he affected as a symbol of his majesty. Goldsmith regained consciousness for a moment, during which he was vaguely aware of being stomped by several pairs of expensive shoes, including those of Bokassa and of one of his sons, Sylvestre. Then Goldsmith passed out again. When he came to, it was eighteen hours later and he was eighty miles away, in Abattoir No. 2, on the condemned row in Ngaragba, handcuffed and bleeding from a dozen places. It was the same cell where a year earlier Bokassa's son-in-law Fidel Obrou had spent his last hours. Goldsmith found a message that Obrou had scratched on one of the walls: They're coming to shoot me this morning, I pray God will have mercy on my soul and that people will look after my family.

Goldsmith was there for a month. A particular sequence of sounds—first terrible screams, then a sharp crack, then silence—would become engraved on his mind. After a week, conditions improved—his meals were brought from the Safari Hotel—and after about a month he was taken back to Berengo, where Bokassa, in the course of a three-hour speech, mostly about himself, told Goldsmith he now considered him a member of the family and offered to make him his personal journalist. He could name his own salary. Goldsmith wasn't interested. Then Bokassa kissed him three times and put him on a plane to Paris.

Later that year Bokassa crowned himself emperor. He had been carefully building to this moment. In 1972 he had made himself president for life. (Each time he went to France he asked, What is an emperor, what is a king, what is a sage? Some think he got the order wrong because he skipped right from president to emperor without ever being king.) In 1974 he became field marshal. By then he was already minister of the interior, defense, agriculture, trade, industry, mines, transportation, civil aviation and aeronautics—and the recipient of thirty-two self-awarded national orders, including first engineer, first farmer, and best soccer player. He could truly say, *"L'état, c'est moi."*

Bokassa's number-one hero was Napoleon. At the Ciné Club in downtown Bangui he screened old movies about Napoleon and studied them carefully. He got the two-hundred-year-old firm of Guiselin, which had embroidered Napoleon's uniforms, to make thirteen outfits for his coronation, including an ermine and velvet robe with a 39-foot train whose 785,000 pearls and 1,220,000 crystal beads took 16,000 seamstress-hours to sew on, and he scheduled his enthronement for December 4—the 173rd anniversary of Napoleon's coronation. The ceremony cost around $25 million, a third of the C.A.R.'s annual budget and all of France's aid for that year. If the bill was footed by French taxpayers, most of the money returned to private French hands. Lanvin made the empress's coronation gown. The imperial crown, by Arthus Bertrand of Paris, was topped with a 138-carat diamond and was worth $2 million; the scepter and the diadem upped the total cost of the jewelry to $5 million.

Giscard contributed twenty diesel Citroëns and sixty air-conditioned limousines for the celebration, even though his relationship with Bokassa had been cooling since the previous fall, perhaps because Bokassa was moving close to the Libyan camp. That October, during a visit by Qaddafi to Bangui, Bokassa had announced that he had converted to Islam and was henceforth to be known as Salah-addin Ahmad Bokassa. But the following December he abandoned his new faith, because it was incompatible with his plans to be crowned emperor in the Catholic cathedral in Bangui—and because his conversion had been contingent on funds promised by Qaddafi that were not forthcoming.

In any case, no Western head of state, no African leader, neither Giscard nor Qaddafi, not even Mobutu, came to the coronation. It was a ridiculous extravaganza which the country, among the twenty-five poorest in the world, could ill afford. Africans were acutely embarrassed. "It will set our image back twenty years," said one African diplomat.

AT THE CLIMAX of the coronation ceremony, Bokassa sat on an enormous golden eagle throne—the wings looming over him had a thirteen-and-a-half-foot span—and swore to defend the constitution of 1959 (which was, in fact, still suspended). When I was wandering around in the now crumbling stadium, I found in a gutted room, cast off to one side, the remains of the eagle throne. The gold was gone, the eight hundred gilded feathers had been plucked by vandals, and it was just a cast-iron skeleton, eaten away by corrosion and rust.

Bokassa's empire lasted less than two years. The massacre of schoolchildren in 1979 was the last straw for his foreign supporters. Bokassa had decreed that all schoolchildren must have uniforms—not only because he was obsessed with uniforms but because his family owned the only uniform factory in the country—and in January there was a peaceful demonstration against the edict by several hundred children of middle-class civil servants whom Bokassa hadn't paid in months, and who couldn't afford the uniforms. Bokassa personally passed out ammunition to soldiers—since the attempt on his life by Obrou, the military hadn't been allowed to have loaded rifles—and gave the order to fire into the crowd. About a dozen children were killed.

On April 19 a group of mostly primary-school children from the *quartier* of Lakounga threw stones at his car. This lèse-majesté could not be countenanced. One hundred and eighty kids were rounded up and thrown into three cells at Ngaragba. I talked to a survivor who told me that it was so hot in his cell that by two o'clock in the afternoon, when he was released because his father was in the military, several six-year-olds with him had suffocated. That night around eight o'clock—ignoring the sobbing entreaties of parents outside the prison—Bokassa stalked in. The children were brought out. Yelling, "I'll teach you to shout Death to the Emperor," he split open the heads of a half-dozen of them with his ebony cane. Then he said to Mokwa, "You finish the job," and stalked out. Only twenty-seven of the children survived.

News of the second massacre reached Amnesty International, and it caused a global outrage. In May, at the Franco-African summit, Giscard was told by other African leaders that Bokassa must go. While he was in Tripoli trying once again to get money from Qaddafi, a thousand crack French paratroopers known as *barracudas*—red berets, camouflage fatigues tucked into combat boots, automatic weapons—took Camp de Roux, the presidential residence, seized the radio station, and proclaimed the end of the empire. David Dacko was awakened in the middle of the night in Paris, told he was president again, and flown to Bangui. *Barracudas* broke into Kolongo and found the torso of Massangue.

There was acute embarrassment in France; extraordinary efforts were made to temper the stories about Bokassa's excesses. Dacko said, "The people might not understand the meaning of cannibalism," and Leopold Senghor, the president of Senegal, said, "Europeans simply don't understand cannibalism." Other *barracudas* stormed the Berengo Palace. Fourteen thousand rough diamonds and two thousand cut ones, some of them up to twenty carats, disappeared.

Jubilant crowds tore down the large statue of Bokassa from its pedestal in the central plaza of Bangui. Bokassa himself flew to Paris, but France wouldn't take him. He sat on the runway for several days, until arrangements were made for the Ivory Coast to give him asylum. He would be a guest in President Houphouët-Boigny's palace in Abidjan for four years, marrying a charming Ivoirienne named Augustine and staying drunk, sometimes for days. Like Ferdinand Marcos, he was just waiting for the signal to return to his country. His bags were packed and ready. Every morning at five he would tune in Radio France Internationale to see if the moment had arrived. In interviews he railed against Giscard, "who took my wife Catherine as his mistress and sent troops to prevent my return to my country." As he saw it, "everyone was jealous because I had an empire and they did not, so they conspired to overthrow me." He claimed, however, that he had "neither the ambition nor the intention of returning to power."

Unable to roast Giscard, he did his best to ruin him. In his memoirs, *Ma Vérité*, ghost-written by the tenant of one of his châteaux, Roger Holeindre, Bokassa said he had to arrange an abortion for Catherine, whom he alleged Giscard had knocked up (a charge Giscard continues to deny). Giscard successfully prevented publication of the book and the entire run of thirty thousand copies was destroyed. He could not stop Bokassa from telling *Le Canard Enchaîné* about all the diamonds Bokassa gave him over the years, which caused a tremendous scandal in France.

In 1980 Bokassa was tried *in absentia* and sentenced to death on eight charges, including embezzling diamonds and massacring the children. The evidence of cannibalism was not ironclad. Then, on September 1, 1981, Dacko was deposed again in a bloodless coup, and General André Kolingba was installed as president. Kolingba is widely believed to be a puppet of the French, and the French head of his six-hundred-man security guard, forty-five-year-old Colonel Jean-Claude Mansion, to be the one really in charge.

On November 26, 1983, twelve mercenaries and a group of supporters led by the French writer Roger Delpey flew to Abidjan and tried to pick up Bokassa, intending to take him to Bangui and restore him to power. But Ivoirien troops, tipped off by French intelligence, surrounded the plane. Houphouët-Boigny was incensed, and he threw Bokassa out of the country, along with fifteen of his children, Augustine, and twenty other women. They took up residence, although the French were hardly enthusiastic about it, at Hardricourt, Bokassa's château near Paris.

Bokassa was profoundly unhappy in France. He complained of having only his military pension of six thousand francs a month to live on. The telephones, water, and electricity at the château were frequently cut off for nonpayment. Three of his children were picked up for shoplifting. Bokassa said they were stealing sausages because they had nothing to eat (they actually stole perfume and records); he refused to bail them out, and they were sent to a state home. How much of his financial miseries were *pour la galerie*, it is impossible to say. Journalists wrote of Bokassa during this period as a sad, broken man. A neighbor described him as "a very considerate man with the most charming manners, and very fond of his children."

In 1984 Bokassa tried to get back to the Central African Republic with false identification papers, but he was foiled by a sharp-eyed clerk. He complained of being held prisoner in his château and denied the right to travel. Then on October 23, 1986, Bokassa escaped from Hardricourt with Augustine, five kids, and eight bags of luggage, eluding his guards by going up a one-way street the wrong way, an unexpected move—the guards were unaware that racing up one-way streets, sending people diving out of the way, was a favorite sport of his in Bangui. After flying from Brussels to Rome under the name Christian Sole, he boarded a flight to Bangui.

Why would he want to return when he had been sentenced to death? Some say that he had made bad business deals and had become involved with crooks, and really had no money, or that he was old and tired and just wanted to go home and die. Shortly before leaving, he told a reporter, "I am a black man and I want to live where it is warm, in the country where I was born. I cannot bear another winter here." Others say that he kept getting letters from old supporters telling him the people wanted him, that he was convinced he would be welcomed back with open arms, that it would be like Napoleon returning from Elba. Others say murky French politics are at the bottom of it. Or that certain parties—like a shady Belgian brunette who had made a lot of money in diamonds when Bokassa was in power —wanted him back and set up his return. Perhaps, as one Central African put it, it was just *un geste de folie*. His defense would be that he had come back to vindicate himself before his people, that he was unaware of all of the details of what had gone on during his regime, yet was willing to assume moral if not penal responsibility for them.

A number of M'Baka tribesmen waiting for him at the airport were hustled off with a manifesto for a new government under Bokassa before he arrived. The majority of Central Africans would have liked to tear him limb from limb, but Colonel Mansion gave orders that he was not to be touched. When Bokassa stepped out of the plane, he found himself looking down the barrels of the *barracudas'* rifles. Augustine was sent back to Paris, and he was imprisoned in the cellar of the Camp de Roux.

THE MOST IMPORTANT thing that happened in the fifty-third session of the *procès Bokassa* was a brilliant maneuver by Szpiner and Gibault. They persuaded the president of the court to agree that Jouanneau, the French lawyer for the C.A.R., had no standing in the trial and couldn't testify. I would have expected Jouanneau to have been a little irritated, but he wasn't. He and his adversaries had crossed paths many times before, and they were the best of friends. At dinner with all three of them that night, I asked Gibault if his conscience bothered him. "No, not at all," he said. "It's the job of a lawyer to defend his client, just as it is a doctor's job to cure the sick. Besides, for a lawyer, this is a magnificent trial." Szpiner was equally enthusiastic. "This trial is an example for all Africa, for the world," he said. "It is one of the very few times an African head of state has been held accountable for his actions. Since Nuremberg there have been two big trials. The one of the generals in Argentina, and the second is this."

How was it going to end? I asked Gibault. "Well," he said, "in the beginning it looked bad for us, but it's looking better and better. The prosecution is very badly prepared, riddled with incompetence. They aren't subpoenaing witnesses, they're just counting on them to show up. I think we'll get Bokassa off on most of the charges for lack of evidence."

Jouanneau hadn't come to testify. His case was separate —a series of financial actions in Europe. "Realistically," he told me, "only the château and the plane [which he had slapped liens on] are recoverable. We can't touch the jewels or the Swiss bank accounts. We could if we could prove the money had been transferred to Switzerland illegally, but under Swiss law it was legal because Bokassa was the head of state and he could do whatever he wanted. Catherine took the crown with her before the coup. She is in Geneva, selling off one diamond at a time. She must be living very well."

I asked Gibault and Szpiner if they were being paid to represent Bokassa, or were they doing it *pro bono, pour la gloire,* or perhaps on spec? Gibault said, "Ah, that is a question I never answer." (Jouanneau said he had been working part-time for the

C.A.R. for a year, but he had no contract and had seen no money. The republic was broke, he said, and waiting for money from France. But he and I flew back to Paris together, and I happened to notice that when the customs officer at Charles De Gaulle opened his valise it contained a huge package of *centrafricain* bank notes. Sheepishly, Jouanneau confessed, "They finally paid me.")

WEDNESDAY THERE WAS no trial, so I hired a jeep and a driver and went down to the virgin forest in the prefecture of Lobaye, where some twenty-five thousand Baminga Pygmies live. I was hoping to tape some of their yodeling, which they do in groups, each one singing a different series of cascading notes. It is some of the most haunting music on earth. I was anxious to get away from the trial and out of Bangui. I knew that just hanging around the Sofitel and the Palais de Justice was giving me a distorted view of the country. Eighty percent of the Central Africans are still subsistence farmers—Fourth World, Fifth World, really, tribal agriculturists who are not in contact with even the limited modernity of Bangui. Their villages are the real Central African Republic.

We set out at five in the morning, doing eighty m.p.h. the whole way on one of the three paved roads outside the capital. It went to Berengo. A teenage girl at the gate who was flipping through a French sex magazine let us in, and we took a quick tour of the palace, which, like Kolongo, is in ruins.

We drove on past Bokassa's coffee and manioc plantations and palm groves, now abandoned and reverting to jungle. In M'Baiki, the biggest town in the area, we stopped for coffee at the market, where handsome M'Baka women in colorful *tissus* sat on platforms before piles of onions, racks of smoked goat ribs, beetle grubs. I asked one if I could take her picture. She said, *"Ça n'intéresse pas,"* not unless you pay me. "What do you think we are? Dogs?" "Who said you were dogs?" I asked. "If you came to my country I'd let you take my picture and you wouldn't have to pay. I mean this in friendship. Besides if I had to pay for every picture I took I'd be broke." Her face creased with humor. "Take the children, then," she said. They lined up eagerly.

The forest beyond M'Baiki is in various stages of disturbance. Only the biggest trees—umbrella and cannonball trees, with immense spreading crowns—have been left standing. As the road twisted and turned, we passed eight-foot-high termite castles, neatly swept bare earth plazas with thatch huts on them, smoldering plots where the forest has been reduced to white ashes except for the charred remnants of a few trees. We drove through Mokinda, David Dacko's village. We stopped where several men had felled a tree across the road as a sort of impromptu toll to extort money from passing vehicles. The driver wasn't about to put up with this outrageous scam, and he let them have it. They moved the tree, and we drove on.

The next village was full of people. The ferryman who would take us across the river flagged us down and got in the car. Everybody was getting vaccinated, he said, but he didn't know what for. Soon we arrived at the Loko, a silent green river spilling through the forest. We drove onto a big, twenty-ton ferry, with room for a dozen cars, more business than it got in a day. Thinking I'd take a dip, and worried about bilharzia (a snail-borne parasite), I asked the ferryman if there were any diseases in the water. He said the biggest danger was men who turned into crocodiles. Spectacular butterflies swarmed the banks. The butterflies of Central Africa are disappearing. Making pictures with their wings has become an art in Bangui. There is an amazing portrait of Reagan in the lobby of the American Embassy made entirely of butterfly wings. But who had any pity left for the butterflies?

Civilization had ended at the river. On the other side we

were *en pleine forêt,* which used to be full of gorillas, the ferryman told us. You never saw them now. Hornbills coasted over the trees. Women hurried along the road carrying manioc roots in wicker baskets with tumplines. It was only a couple of miles to the Congo, and there the road ended. After that, it was just foot trails for weeks.

In the village of Mongoumba we stopped at the École d'Intégration des Pygmées, and from there it was a ten-minute walk to the Pygmy village of Sakábu. The men there were taller than the Efe men I had met in the Ituri Forest. They had pointed teeth, and wavy scars on their abdomens. They sang some rousing camp music, which I taped. But where are the women? I asked. They left this morning to catch fish, one of them told me. A young M'Bati man, Patrice Topessoua, offered to take us to them. We drove on to within a mile of the Congo border, stopping, at Patrice's suggestion, to buy corn liquor. Then we parked and Patrice led us into some dark, majestic woods, with giant millipedes measuring the leaf litter and butterflies flashing in shafts of sunlight that had broken through the canopy. Patrice pointed to a place on a tree where the Pygmies had gouged the bark, which they used to treat stomachaches. We stopped at a heap of leaves which he said was called a *zaú.* Here two Pygmies made love, he explained, and when they finished they marked the spot with a handful of leaves. Everybody who passes here has to grab a handful of leaves, spit on it, and throw it on the pile. The *zaú* is an offering to the god of the Pygmies, the genie of the forest. It brings luck net-hunting for antelope. We each picked up a bunch of leaves, spat on it, and added it to the *zaú.* Soon we came to a small village of mixed M'Bati and Baminga. A toddler screamed in terror at the sight of me, and ran to hide under his mother's *tissu.* Evidently he'd never seen a white man. Huge tree-snail shells littered the edge of the village.

We continued. After five minutes we began to hear a loud

hum, a joyous human roar, an excited hullabaloo. Then we burst onto an incredible scene. Hundreds of people—Pygmies, M'Bati, and members of a riverine tribe, the Mondjombo—were wading in the swamp, whose water they had impounded in a series of dams. Some were removing the water with bowls and tubs. Others were filtering the mud with wicker baskets and taking little wriggling fish from the baskets and wrapping them in packets of leaves. Patrice showed the Pygmy women the corn liquor and asked if they would sing for us, and all the Pygmies traipsed back to the village, where some of the women put on grass skirts. One tucked some leaves in the back of her fiber G-string in a festive gesture. Patrice passed around the liquor, fifty Pygmies took a swig, the rhythm section (three men on two long drums and a plastic oil can) set up; the women formed a chorus line, a sidling circle, a choochoo train in which they remained locked for an hour, their bodies glistening with sweat, their eyes glazed as if in a spell, blended sounds of unearthly beauty coming from their mouths. This is the first time anybody like you has ever visited them and they are happy to dance for you, Patrice said. They seemed oblivious to the question of Bokassa's crimes, and to have been unaffected by his reign of terror. The whole thing seemed to have washed right over them.

MY LAST AFTERNOON in the Central African Republic, I had to make a choice. Should I go to the trial, and listen to more of Bokassa's lying? There was a new expression in Bangui: You lie like Bokassa. Or should I get in a little Third World golf at the Golf Club de Bangui with my new friend Alain Georges, director of the local branch of the Pasteur Institute, and an authority on AIDS.

Bangui's fifteen-hole course was unlike any I had ever played. It took twenty stabs to plant the flexible tee Georges handed me into the gravelly, lateritic soil. I drove with his son's three wood and the ball sailed over a frangipani. Then it took a tremendous bounce, then another, and vanished in the swimming heat. I could see that overclubbing was going to be a problem. Once you made the green, however, your ball wasn't going anywhere, because the green was brown sand—the way greens were in the early days of the game. Your caddie simply smoothed a path to the pin with a rakelike board, and you putted straight for the cup. There were no breaks to agonize over.

A bearded forty-one-year-old who doesn't get to play as much as he would like, Georges was into golf mainly for the walk, the Zen of the game, and the friendly competition—as I was. After a pleasant but undistinguished round, we repaired to the clubhouse for a tall, cold bottle of the local beer, Super, and were soon joined by Martin Yando, the chief of President Kolingba's cabinet, who had been playing just behind us. I asked Yando how he thought the trial was going. He said it was a turning point in the history of the republic. It showed to the world that justice and due process had returned to the C.A.R., that even people like Bokassa had the right to be defended. It was also a catharsis, an exorcism, a chance for the traumatized population to free itself of the anguish that remained from the years of terror and to give way to grief.

Did he have a sense of the verdict? "It must not be a public vendetta," he said. Not, then, like Nguema's execution in 1979. (Nguema, who killed at least 50,000 of his countrymen and turned Equatorial Guinea into a virtual concentration camp, was executed *au fur et à mesure*, according to a Central African I'm not sure I believe: first his fingers were cut off, then an arm, and each day the journalists whose profession he had made a capital offense would come to him and ask, "How does it feel now, what you did?") "But to tell you the truth," Yando added, "I have no idea how it will go. You must remember that this is Africa."

In June, Bokassa was sentenced to death. Because so many

M'Baka are still in the government, however, it was widely thought that the sentence would not be carried out and that he would be allowed to emigrate to Morocco, which had welcomed the Shah. (Idi Amin is still alive and well in Saudi Arabia, where he has reportedly become deeply religious.) Szpiner and Gibault's appeal for a retrial on the constitutional grounds that a former head of state can only be tried on charges of treason was rejected by the Central African supreme court, and the death sentence was upheld. The latest word is that Bokassa's sentence was commuted to life, and he is still imprisoned in the basement of the presidential palace, on the hill above the Sofitel. One wonders what kind of parties are going on up there.

IN SEARCH OF
THE SOURCE OF
AIDS

Thou shalt not be afraid for the terror by night; nor for the arrow that flieth by day; Nor for the pestilence that walketh in darkness; nor for the destruction that wasteth at noonday. A thousand shall fall at thy side, and ten thousand at thy right hand; but it shall not come nigh thee. Only with thine eyes shalt thou behold. . . .

—Psalm 91

In the past two decades one of the fondest boasts of medical science has been the conquest of infectious disease, at least in the wealthy countries of the industrialized world. The advent of retroviruses with the capacity to cause extraordinarily complex and devastating disease has exposed that claim for what it was: hubris. Nature is never truly conquered. The human retroviruses and their intricate interrelationship with the human cell are but one example of that fact. Indeed, perhaps conquest is the wrong metaphor to describe our relationship to nature, which not only surrounds but in the deepest sense also constitutes our being.

—Robert Gallo,
Scientific American

Civil war has raged in Uganda for the past twenty years, and AIDS is loose on the land, but the country's terrible suffering isn't apparent in the placid, bucolic landscape rolling past the car window. The rutted road runs on over a lush, undulating plateau spattered with banana groves and gleaming, zinc-roofed huts. Every so often we part a herd of lyre-horned Ankole cattle, or a woman of the local tribe, the Baganda, steps gracefully out of the way of the car, turns, and looks at us frankly. Most of the women are in their native dress, called *bodingi*, a cinched, one-piece outfit whose winged shoulders and bold colors and patterns make them seem like gaudy butterflies. We begin to meet increasing numbers of young men on bicycles coming up from Lake Victoria—alone, in pairs, in groups of six or seven, with the enormous fishtails flopping out of wicker baskets. The fish are called *imputa*. The young men are taking them to Masaka, a city we left miles back, where they can sell them for two hundred bob apiece—less than two dollars, a honest day's work.

We are headed for Kasensero, a small village on Lake Victoria's southwestern shore. Kasensero is in Uganda's Rakai district, which some believe is the place where AIDS originated. Edward, a big, muscular young man, is at the wheel of the Land-

Rover, deftly dodging potholes. Baker, the mechanic, who wears a floppy hat and a perpetual smirk, is in the back seat. Neither of them speaks much English.

In the fall of 1982, seventeen people in Kasensero came down with fulminating AIDS, the first reported cases of the disease in Uganda. The inhabitants of Kasensero are for the most part smugglers who bring in things like sheets of roofing and plastic plates from Tanzania to sell in the cities of Masaka and Kampala. According to the Ugandan ministry of health they also brought in AIDS. "The smugglers brought the problem over," a man there had told me. The people in the surrounding villages and the smugglers themselves thought the disease was a form of divine retribution. "When they died it was believed to be a punishment for the illicit trade they were engaged in," the official had explained.

According to another version, the smugglers were done in by witchcraft. They were made sick by Tanzanians they had cheated. The people of Rakai began to call the illness thieves' disease, but when some of the thieves' women started to waste away and die, the people thought of a new name: Slim. According to my source, Slim moved steadily north, traveling about fifty miles a year. By 1985 it had reached Kampala, the capital.

Ugandans insist that the disease, whatever name it goes by, is not theirs. And in fact maybe Kasensero isn't where it started at all (there is evidence of AIDS as early as 1972 in northwestern Uganda, in the Nile Province, Idi Amin's homeland), but at some level, perhaps only mythical, Kasensero is the font of AIDS. "All the scientific signposts point to an origin in Africa, somewhere around the region of Lake Victoria," said Robert Gallo, the leading American AIDS researcher. It is the only rural part of Africa with a raging epidemic.

The road leads on and on through marsh and pasture. We are dead on the equator, and the sun is incredibly hot. I imagine myself a latter-day Ponce de León, searching for the Fountain of Death. Or as Captain John Speke, about to discover Lake Victoria, the source of the White Nile. How curious it would be, I think, if the source of the Nile and the source of AIDS prove to be one and the same, that vast teeming lake deep in the dangerous heart of darkest Africa.

We pick up a couple and give them a lift to the next village, Kyotera. Baker tells me, "They burned one [a Slim victim] yesterday in their village, and where they were going so many have died" that *bazungu*, whites, have come to study the situation. I ask how many are so many and Baker says very many. Having been through this often enough before in the Third World, I know it is futile to expect reliable figures. Numbers are white man's business, a temperate-zone precision trip. Here they are flourishes, thrown out for effect. The figures are figurative. I ask how the couple think Slim is transmitted. "Mainly by sex but sometimes by witchcraft against debt welchers," they say. We pull into the neatly swept bare-earth plaza of Kyotera and get out. I am surrounded by a dozen children, my mere presence enough to send them into gales of laughter. Baker and Edward buy several huge green hands of *matoke*, cooking bananas, to take home to their families. Kyotera is one of the small trading centers in Rakai where men from other villages and local women inevitably come into contact and often trade venereal diseases.

Several miles farther on we come to a roadblock manned by ragged soldiers—Resistance council members, Baker calls them—who are lounging under a tree and roasting *matoke* on an open fire. I ask Baker what the roadblock is for and he says to combat smuggling and to stop antigovernment fellows from bringing in arms from Tanzania. The soldiers slip back the pole and we proceed, flushing swarms of lemon-barred swallowtail butterflies from puddles in the road. In the village of Kyebe we stop and walk uphill to a small, tidy clinic. A dozen women are seated on benches. There is a stench of diarrhea. Someone is pounding a drum in the adjacent banana grove. Who's in charge? I ask. He's in there, I am told. I look into the dark dispensary. The doctor comes out, coughing. He sees me, pulls himself together, and flashes a winsome, white-toothed smile. He is in his late twenties, with large shiny eyes, a good-looking chap. Except that he is very weak and wasted. There is no flesh on his arms. He cannot stand alone, and props himself up against the door as we talk. His assistant tells me that there are eighteen hundred people in Kyebe and "we bury every day about six. This month we treated about twenty, and more than thirty died." The numbers problem again.

I give the doctor a letter of introduction from a clinic I visited the day before. He reads it and says apologetically, "I'm afraid I can't take you around. There are only two of us here and many patients."

"You don't look so good yourself," I say.

"Just a cough," he replies cheerily.

Obviously he can't go anywhere. He's got it. Shit, I realized, even the doctor's got it. He has maybe two months to live.

THE DISCOVERY, BEGINNING in 1983, that an epidemic of AIDS more advanced than anywhere else in the world is raging in Central Africa, and that the main mode of transmission is heterosexual intercourse, created panic in the United States and Europe, where the disease is mainly confined to small, identifiable risk groups—male homosexuals, IV drug users, hemophiliacs. Many Western scientists are convinced that the disease started in Central Africa, that it has been there longer than anywhere else, and that our epidemic will therefore over time come to resemble theirs, i.e., that the plague will spread into the "general" population of Europe and America. They claim that what is happening in Africa is a nightmare vision of the future of the West.

Many Africans are equally convinced that AIDS was introduced to them by Europeans or Americans. Some Zaïrois say it was brought in by rich American sports fans who came to Kinshasa for the Ali-Foreman fight in 1974. Others say it was introduced in canned food donated by the developed countries. A television campaign in Zaire urges that to avoid getting the deadly disease it is only necessary to abide by President Mobutu's principle of *authenticité* and to "eat African." Theories abound about an artificial origin: that it arose from a lab mutation of the yellow-fever vaccine or from an accident in a recombinant DNA experiment; or the Soviet theory, once widely spread and since disavowed, that the virus was developed in a germ-warfare lab in Maryland and deliberately unleashed by the Pentagon.

The same geographical buck passing took place five centuries ago, when the last great sexual scourge, syphilis, broke out in the West—among the soldiers of the French king, Charles VIII, who had been laying siege to the city of Naples in 1494. Four years later, Vasco da Gama's sailors took the disease to India. By the time it reached China and Japan, in 1509, millions had died along the way. As the pandemic raged, there was a lot of finger-pointing. The French blamed the Italians for unleashing the plague. The Italians blamed the Turks. The Old World blamed the New, and the New World blamed the Old. No one wanted to be the source of syphilis. And the source was never determined.

The problem with identifying the source of AIDS is compounded by the fact that there are at least two viruses that seem to produce acquired immune deficiency in humans: HIV-1, which was isolated at the Pasteur Institute in Paris in 1983 and is now being reported from 127, or three-quarters, of the world's countries; and HIV-2, isolated two years later, also at the Pasteur

Institute. Many scientists believe that other viruses will turn up. The case for an African origin of HIV-2 is fairly strong. One strain is seventy percent genetically identical with a virus found in green monkeys, the most common monkeys on the continent, so it appears to have an ancestor and a natural reservoir in Africa. The theory is that some time ago it crossed over from the monkeys to humans. The ancestor of HIV-1, however, has yet to be found in Africa, or anywhere.

The second AIDS virus seems to have been around somewhat longer than HIV-1, and yet for reasons that are hotly debated it has produced far fewer cases of AIDS. The great majority of cases and the highest rates of people who test positive for the virus come from a small, destitute country below Senegal called Guinea-Bissau, the former Portuguese Guinea. It is possible that AIDS has been killing people in Guinea-Bissau for a long time, but that nobody knew it because the disease had not been identified. No one would have suspected that the untreatable diarrhea and the tuberculosis that were killing people were caused by a new virus. "We have had diarrhea and tuberculosis for thousands of years," Venâncio Furtado, Guinea-Bissau's director-general of public health, told me. "This is an old disease with a new name that was given quickly—perhaps too quickly. I think there are thousands of these kinds of viruses. The first ones come out and they put the blame on Africa."

A virus is a parasite of cells, a much smaller freeloader than single-celled parasites like amoebas. I picked up a good nutshell definition in Nairobi, in a high-school reader called *Rainbow* that had been laid out for sale on a sidewalk with all kinds of other reading matter. There was a section in the reader called "AIDS: The Facts," and in the section there was a box that said "A virus is a packet of genetic information wrapped in a covering made of protein. It is very small, about one tenthousandth the size of a human body cell. Viruses do not eat.

They do not respire. They cannot reproduce without help from another cell. Because of this, some scientists are not even sure they are alive."

New viruses are appearing and disappearing all the time, or perhaps more accurately, reaching critical enough intensity in human populations that they come to our attention. This is especially true in the tropics, particularly, it would seem, in Africa. "The Leakey theory of life beginning here does not only apply to human beings," one scientist told me. "Africa is the perfect incubator for all life." All forms of life have been evolving longer in Africa than elsewhere. There is a greater proliferation of pathogenic microorganisms than in the New World tropics.

In 1959, for instance, a new human disease, called *O'nyong nyong* fever (or monkey pox, literally "bone-breaker," because it caused aches and pains as well as fever and headache), appeared in Uganda, probably as a result of mosquitoes transferring an arborvirus from monkeys to humans. The disease spread quickly, but its effects were mild, recovery was complete, and it soon disappeared as mysteriously as it had come.

Eight years later, twenty-five lab workers in Marburg, Germany, came down with hemorrhagic fever (fever accompanied by bleeding) after handling infected tissue from green monkeys imported from Uganda. A quarter of them died. Sexual transmission was documented in one case. The Marburg virus still claims a victim or two from time to time. In 1975 an Austrian traveler died in South Africa, apparently after contracting the virus in Zimbabwe. Five years later a French engineer died of it in Kenya, and his physician came down with the fever but recovered.

In 1969, another hemorrhagic fever killed two nurses in the hospital of a small Nigerian town called Lassa. The Lassa fever virus was traced to rats in and around the huts in the vicinity. It could have been transmitted by their urine and excreta on food left out on tables. Once a person was infected, he or she could pass it on sexually. Lassa fever still breaks out from time to time, usually in West Africa.

In 1976 still another hemorrhagic fever surfaced in two places within a short distance of each other, first in the southern Sudan, and then in Yambuku, in northwestern Zaire. Over half the cases were fatal. The fever was named after a local river, the Ebola. Its natural reservoir is not known. It was spread by unsterilized needles in the hospitals there, sexually, and by ritual contact with the corpses of previous fever victims during burial. An epidemiologist brought in from the Centers for Disease Control in Atlanta banned local funerals, ordered the corpses of the victims to be unceremoniously buried, and quarantined the infected survivors. Within weeks, the disease disappeared as mysteriously as it had come.

In 1983 an epidemic of hemorrhagic conjunctivitis started in West Africa and swept the tropics. It spread to Brazil (where it infected half the population of Belém, a big city at the mouth of the Amazon); to Panama and Malaysia. The symptoms were inflamed, bloodshot eyes. The victims thought they were going blind. But the condition usually cleared up after a week; there were only a few cases of neurological involvement. After a while the epidemic died down, the virus just went away, apparently mutating out of existence.

The Lassa, Ebola, and Marburg viruses are evanescent hemorrhagic fever viruses—rural diseases that usually don't survive outside their area. Their incubation period is two or three days or weeks. Their victims die or recover. Then the viruses drop out of sight. You don't hear about them unless the number of their victims becomes too large to ignore. Their ecological niches are not understood, but their primary role in nature is not to infect man. They infect man by accident, and when that happens the infection can be serious.

The human immunodeficiency viruses, HIV-1 and HIV-2, however, are a different kettle of fish. The HIVs have a latency period of years, and once they infect someone, the infection is apparently lifelong. In these respects and in their mode of transmission, by blood or sex, they are more like the hepatitis B virus, but HBV is a lot more stable. You can boil it and still not kill it. Perhaps some time ago, within the last hundred years, HIV-1 crossed over from monkeys, as HIV-2 may have. Or perhaps it evolved from HIV-2. (There is growing evidence of what one scientist calls a "cloud" of strains between HIV-1 and HIV-2.) Or perhaps, as some think, two previously isolated human retroviruses came into contact during the turmoil in Africa during the seventies and produced a third, lethal one. It could have mutated frequently and rapidly, faster perhaps than even the flu virus—adapting to growth in sexual fluids, gaining virulence.

It is also possible that a fully pathogenic virus could have percolated in some isolated rural population for years without being detected. The deaths it caused would have been seen as ordinary cases of diarrhea, fever, pneumonia, meningitis, cancer, or whatever. Or the virus could have been established in a population that had a natural resistance to it, as Luc Montagnier at the Pasteur Institute has suggested.

During the late sixties and early seventies, the populations of eleven cities in Central Africa mushroomed to over a million, and there was tremendous upheaval—civil wars, rebellions, armies marching over the landscape. It was then that HIV could have been swept out of its rural hiding place and taken into the urban African setting, where new levels of promiscuity and a breakdown of health services enabled it to spread quickly, at the same time that the sexual revolution and a flourishing subculture of gay bars and bathhouses were providing an amplification system for it in America and Europe. Special local conditions—the ongoing war in Uganda, the good road system in Zambia, the density of population in Rwanda, the sexual anarchy in Zaire—caused it to be especially amplified in these countries.

There are a number of rather compelling circumstantial reasons for thinking that HIV-1 originated in Central Africa. For one thing the African strains are genetically more diverse and they seem to have been evolving longer, i.e., to be older than the ones found in Europe and America. By far the highest rates of HIV-1 infection in the world are found in Central Africa, also suggesting that the virus has been there longer. The first cases in Europe, in the late seventies, occurred among Africans or Europeans who had been to Africa. (An African connection to the American cases is a lot harder to establish.)

Then there are the clinical features of the syndrome. Early workers with AIDS in Europe and the U.S. were struck by how "African" the disease pattern seemed. In the early cases, one of the main killers was Kaposi's sarcoma, primarily an African cancer, rare in the West. The diarrhea, the infestation of intestinal parasites like *Entamoeba, Giardia, Cryptosporidium, Ascaris, Trichuris, Salmonella*, and *Shigella* that ravage AIDS victims are common in poor rural Africa, but not in the developed world. Burkitt's lymphoma, another of the opportunistic AIDS cancers, is rare in a nontropical setting, and most widespread in the so-called lymphoma belt of Africa, fifteen degrees north and south of the equator, which is also the endemic area of Kaposi's sarcoma.

But is the clinical picture of AIDS really African? Or is it because Africans are immunocompromised that they come down with these diseases, and the moment Westerners are similarly immunocompromised (as the sexually overexerted gay population in North America became in the seventies) they come down with them, too? But, then, if this is the case, why don't all the immunosuppressed populations in the Third World have a clinical profile similar to Africans and Western AIDS victims?

There is more than one way of looking at the outbreak of AIDS in Africa. Some believe that AIDS is a divine scourge, but that is hard to accept, especially since many of its victims are not sinfully promiscuous—children, wives of womanizers, widows, and unwed mothers simply trying to survive. There may be a different teleological explanation, a biological one: that the epidemic arose as nature's way of checking a population that technology and "progress" had enabled to grow unnaturally. Viruses and other disease-causing organisms frequently arise as a control mechanism in populations that experience sudden growth. There is a virus that thins out gypsy moths in New England when they get out of hand, and when raccoons become too numerous in the New York suburbs they begin to get rabies.

It is in the context of the ongoing theater of life, of the contest between microbial parasites and their mammalian hosts, and of nature's intricate systems of checks and balances, that the struggle between AIDS and man is perhaps best understood.

GUINEA-BISSAU

When I arrived in Bissau, the sleepy, steamy capital that was the first stop on my trip into the AIDS heartland, none of my telexes to the ministry of health had gotten through. But at least I was expected at the Hotel 24 do Setembro. The hotel had been a Portuguese officers' barracks during the eleven-year war of independence. It was a strangely austere place, almost like a tropical research center. There were no whores on the premises, as there often are in African hostelries; most of the guests were serious young Scandinavian or Dutch humanitarians working for development agencies, who identified with the socialist ideals of the country's martyred liberator, Amílcar Cabral. In the evening they would sit at separate tables, reading technical papers.

Guinea-Bissau is one of the ten poorest countries in the world. In the five centuries since the Portuguese carved this sliver, the size of Indiana, out of the West African bulge, they did little except enslave the local people and ship them to Cabo Verde and the New World. The only industry they left behind when they finally pulled out in 1974 was a brewery for their soldiers.

In the fourteen years since independence the country has traveled only a short way down the road to modern nation-statehood. It has no private sector, a floating currency that nobody wants, and only two things to sell, cashews and peanuts. Most of its eight hundred thousand or so people live in villages known as *tabancas*; their traditional way of life is remarkably intact. Not all of them speak the colonial dialect, *criolo*, a blend of Portuguese morphology and African phonetics with loan words from both stocks. Only educated people in Bissau speak Portuguese, and I had to rely on them as interpreters to communicate with the others.

The Guineans have a surprising lack of ill feeling toward their former oppressors, and it was to Portugal that they turned in 1978–79 when the first cases of chronic diarrhea, profound weight loss, fever, and tuberculosis and other respiratory ailments, none of which would respond to treatment, began to appear at the Hospital Simão Mendes in Bissau, the largest hospital in the country. Several of the patients were sent to the Hospital Egas Moniz in Lisbon, where they were examined by Dr. Wanda Canas-Ferreira, a virologist at the adjacent Institute of Tropical Medicine and Hygiene. "At first I thought it might be an enterovirus, like polio," she told me when I visited her on the way down to Africa. "But we checked and found nothing. Then in 1981 the first cases of AIDS began to appear in the

U.S. We associated the pathologies, and when the Montagnier lab at the Pasteur Institute isolated [HIV-1], we sent them blood samples from our patients, but they were either negative or only weakly positive. By now we had thirty patients. The first ones had died. Most of them died within two or three years."

The Montagnier lab kept working on the blood samples Canas-Ferreira had sent them, and in 1985 it isolated the second AIDS virus, HIV-2, from two of the Guineans dying far from home at Egas Moniz.

Since then, French, American, Portuguese, Danish, and Italian research teams have been coming to Guinea-Bissau to draw blood from the local people. The results of such sero-surveys become part of the hot global race to find a vaccine. Reports are published in Western scientific journals and released to the Western press. Americans and Europeans can read often-garbled accounts in their morning papers, but the Africans from whom the blood was taken are still kept in the dark about the epidemic that is raging on their continent. At this point, no African country is giving its seropositives the results of their tests. Even prostitutes who test positive for HIV are not told. They return to the streets where they may continue to infect the population. Many scientists, Western and African, are deeply upset about this policy. "Unless you give the patients the results," an American AIDS diagnostician told me, the research is "all for promotion and tenure."

An African health official I asked about the ethics of this policy explained, "We don't tell the seropositive because he is going to get very frightened and upset and is not going to stop transmitting. He may commit suicide—as a number have—or even decide not to die alone and disseminate the disease deliberately. Furthermore, if he's healthy there's no point in telling him, in branding him with a death sentence because there is a good chance that he may be a false positive and not have the virus at all." The false positive rate in Africa is absolutely staggering. The initial test to determine the presence of HIV antibodies, the ELISA, is highly fallible. One scientist estimated that when the ELISA is given to the general population it yields about sixty-six percent false positives; two out of three, in other words, aren't carrying the virus at all.

THERE HAD BEEN problems with foreign journalists, Venâncio Furtado said. He was hunched over his desk at the Office of Public Health, looking up at me balefully. The worst case of "inflammation of information" had occurred when the results of a survey of twenty people from Bissau, five of whom tested positive for HIV-2, were released to the Portuguese press. The next day there were headlines saying that twenty-five percent of the people in Guinea-Bissau had AIDS. Furtado said that other diseases were the big killers—malaria (which attacks two hundred million Africans a year and kills a million children), measles, sleeping sickness, bilharziasis, the twenty-percent infant mortality mainly from gastroenteritis, from *Shigella*, *Salmonella*, and other parasites. "Chernobyl, Bhopal," he said, "these are more frightening." He confirmed that so far the patients and their families were not being told what they had. Most of the public did not know that nasty little microbes were on the loose, threatening to kill them. They still believed the *irãs*, the spirits, were the cause of sickness and death. In some ways, Furtado observed, the viruses had a lot in common with the *irãs*: they were invisible, their existence had to be taken on faith, and one was powerless against them.

"We are moving cautiously, to avoid panic," Furtado said. The government was "on the eve" of making a declaration. Maybe this week, or next week. He ended the interview on a rather deep note: "Western medical science has made many advances, but it has still not discovered the mechanism of consciousness, the secret of the brain. If we knew that secret, if we understood how the brain controls the defense of the organism, we would not be so frustrated by SIDA [the acronym for AIDS in Portuguese, French, and the other Romance languages]. But I am convinced that we will eradicate this disease just as we have conquered smallpox and plague and other epidemics in the past. No propaganda will stop our march."

THAT AFTERNOON I went for a drink with the American ambassador, John Dale Blacken, and I ended up staying for dinner. Guinea-Bissau seems to be one of the few places where we are still popular. Crowds cheer the ambassador when he drives by in his limo flying the Stars and Stripes. It is a quiet post. Outside the compound, which boasts one of the country's six tennis courts, we could hear drums. A circumcision ceremony was in progress. At eleven p.m. it started to pour. Just beyond the patio, no more than fifty feet away, there was a sudden blinding flash followed by a huge boom of such force that I was thrown from the living room sofa, where the ambassador and I were sitting, watching a video cassette of *Bye Bye Brazil*. My first thought was a bomb. Guerrillas are storming the American ambassador's residence. But then a powerful smell of ozone began to seep in through the louvered shutters. Just a lightning bolt.

IN THE MORNING, I walked from the hotel down the road lined with zinc-roofed bungalows. A colony of magnificent lacy-plumed snowy egrets had taken over a huge tree above one of them, and the roof and yard were spattered with their gooey white droppings. The owners seemed to be living with the situation, to be making no effort to drive the birds away. It was a case study in tropical acceptance.

Furtado was waiting in the sweltering heat of his office. "I think it is important for you to visit one of our *curandeiros*, or traditional healers," he said. "They have a profound understanding of the mental aspects of illness and also many good herbal remedies for specific complaints like diarrhea, so there is much to learn from them." He provided me with a letter of introduction to the regional health administrator in the town of Cantchungu and a guide, a young male nurse named José Augusto Sanha.

José Augusto and I flagged a sturdy Renault taxi, and hired it and the driver, a young man named Omaru, for the day. Then we set out on the road to Cantchungu. We were going into the country of the Manjaco, José Augusto told me, one of Guinea-Bissau's dozen tribes. We drove past the shell of a modern highrise hotel, abandoned in mid-construction, either because the builders had run out of money or because hopeless leaks had developed in the roof, or because everybody was on vacation; José Augusto had heard all three explanations. Just outside the city limits we passed an African spitting cobra coiled and swaying on the curb. Fifty yards on, a barefoot boy was running after some goats in the tall grass.

We drove through a steamy lowlands with palm groves and rice paddies, penetrated by tongues of the sea, and at last reached the Rio Mansôa, a gray estuary lined with tall, thick reeds. There was no bridge, and the ferry was stuck in the mud. In three hours the tide would rise and free it. José Augusto said the ferryman had run the ferry aground on purpose because he didn't want to work.

It was not a nice place to have to wait. The heat was unremitting, the filth skin-crawling. I had picked up a transitory low-grade virus, and my nose was stuffed. Several dozen radiantly attired women and children stood or squatted in a group by the ferry landing. Most of the children were wearing necklaces or belts with black leather packets containing fetishes, or *muru*, to protect them from fever, diarrhea, measles, and bad spirits.

We reached Cantchungu in time for a late lunch, and from there were driven by truck for several hours to the village of Caimete, where a famous *curandeiro* has a clinic. On the way we stopped at a rural clinic where a group of pregnant women was being advised on malaria prevention; they were told to cut back the leaves from their houses and to drain stagnant pools where anopheles mosquitoes could breed. "There are different kinds of *curandeiros*," José Augusto told me. "Some are gynecologists, some are dentists. This one specializes in setting broken bones." The road passed between two ancient trees into an earthy compound of mud and thatch huts. The veranda of the longest hut was partitioned with walls of mosquito netting into six cubicles, and in each cubicle there was a cot. There was only one patient. José Augusto said that in the dry season the clinic is full of people. The patient was a woman whose right tibia had been crushed by a two-hundred-liter barrel of cashew wine. She had been here three weeks. In the plaza a tall, grizzled old man was boiling a brew in a ceramic pot. He said it was for mastitis. He was the *curandeiro*. We greeted him and talked about his patient. He told us that when she arrived he went to the *baloba*, the sacred bastion of the *irãs* in the forest, and asked the *irãs* if he could treat her. How did he communicate with the *irãs*? I asked. He sacrificed a rooster. If the testicles were white, as they usually were, the *irãs* approved of her treatment; if they were black, the treatment was refused. The *curandeiro* had then set the bone and wrapped it in a fiber cast slathered with palm oil. José Augusto looked at the job and said it was very good. The woman was a Manjaco. Her abdomen was scored with a linear series of decorative scars.

Ritual scarification is one of the tribal practices that is suspected of playing a role in the spread of AIDS in Africa.*

*The best discussion of this subject is Daniel B. Hrdy's paper, "Cultural Practices Contributing to the Transmission of Human Immunodeficiency Virus in Africa," *Reviews of Infectious Diseases* 9 (1987):1109–19.

The cuts that produce the scars are made during group rites of passage, with a shared, unsterilized instrument such as a hooked thorn or a razor, sometimes with both, as when the skin is lifted by the thorn and then sliced by the razor so that it will heal over with a raised glossy formation of connected tissue overgrowth. Besides decorative scars, medicinal or curative incisions are made on the back or abdomen and the "black blood" or "dirty blood" is sucked out through a cow horn as treatment for malaria, rheumatism, or local pain. Tutsi children in Uganda receive three small parallel cuts on their chest to protect them, like a fetish, from childhood diseases. Some tribes go in for genital tattooing, which entails repeated poking of unsterilized needles into the labia and vaginal wall. The only evidence so far of scarification being implicated in the transmission of AIDS is a study of forty children from two to fourteen years old made in Kinshasa, Zaire, in 1986: a history of scarification was more common in those who were seropositive. But in fact throughout Africa AIDS is markedly absent from this age group, and not noticeably present in the rural areas where scarification is most prevalent, so the practice does not appear to be playing a significant role in transmission. The virus does not survive long when it is exposed on a knife or razor blade.

I asked the *curandeiro* if we could go to the *baloba*. He said no, it's sacred, dangerous. Only people from here can see it. Then I asked him who the *irãs* were. "They are natural beings who appear, powerful beings. Only he who has great art can see them. They come in dreams as a normal person, a man, woman, or child, except that they are white." How does fever come? I asked. "Either from the *irãs* or from *bichos*, little beasts or bugs. The fever that is provoked by *bichos* I seek herbs for. Fever can also come from a *mal vento*, a bad wind, or if a person has worked a lot, or from an enemy." What about diarrhea? "It can come from fever, from eating, or from *bichos*. Children sometimes pass the *bichos* in their stool." He showed me a plant for treating diarrhea that he had just picked. "This one you pound in a mortar, boil, and drink. It only works when it is picked from the *baloba*. If it doesn't work there are two others."

WE REACHED THE Rio Mansôa at ten to nine. The ferryman had said the last ferry left at nine, but it was already gone. We screamed and yelled and blinked our headlights at the other side, and the ferryman blinked back but they didn't come for us. *"Ele nâo tem palavra profissional,"* José Augusto said. "He is not professional, not a man of his word. Omaru, the taximan, said we would have to go around the long way back to Bissau, and he wasn't sure we had enough gas. So we started down a bumpy back road through the forest, coasting with the engine off on downgrades. I asked Omaru if he believed in the *irás*. He was a Fula, a Moslem and not an animist tribe, and he said no. José Augusto, who was Papel, the tribe that predominates in Bissau, said, "They have never come to me but I accept their existence. They never came to me because I am influenced by the culture of the city, which is against everything they know to be true."

However inconvenient it was for us, it was a good thing for the spread of AIDS that there isn't a bridge over the Rio Mansôa, that Guinea-Bissau and West Africa in general aren't linked up by a long-distance international highway system, the way Central and East Africa are. Tradition and poor roads are delaying the spread of the virus here.

The rural Manjaco women in this area have severe constraints placed on their sexual freedom by what José Augusto described as a "system of intimidation." Typically, each Manjaco man has three wives. Each wife is taken to the *irás* and is convinced in a ceremony that she will die if she goes with other men. "Even if she goes to Senegal for ten years," José Augusto assured me. "Or at least she can't play around in the husband's territory."

Our headlights kept illuminating two-and-a-half- or three-foot, low-slung, gray-banded weaseloid carnivores slinking across the road, probably large-spotted genets. I wondered if they had been tested for retroviruses, the peculiar family of viruses to which HIV-1 and HIV-2 belong. Since 1910, when the first retroviruses were discovered, they have been found in chickens, cats, cows, goats, horses, sheep, and monkeys. Robert Gallo and his colleagues at the National Cancer Institute isolated the first human retrovirus in the late seventies. HIV-1 was the third human retrovirus to be identified.

New retroviruses are turning up all the time. Recently, one whose antibodies are similar to those of both HIV-1 and HIV-2 was found in the Amazon by a scientific team headed by Francis Black of Yale, first among the howler monkeys on an island in the Tocantins River, then in a small percentage of Indians, most of whom were women who butchered the monkeys and other game the men brought in. Black told me that his discovery suggests that primate retroviruses have been in existence for at least thirty-five million years, because they are found in both New and Old World species. They have been around, in other words, since well before the appearance of humans. Spider and cebus monkeys have them, too. So do gibbons in Malaysia. "There is a variety of viruses related to AIDS in both humans and monkeys that we are only beginning to decipher," Black told me.

THE FOLLOWING MORNING I drove east into the country of the Fula, Omaru's tribe, which practices both male and female circumcision—another custom that may be conducive to the

spread of AIDS not only because, like the scarification ceremonies, it is a group ritual involving the use of a shared, unsterilized instrument, but because the mutilated tissue of the
women is later prone to tears during intercourse.

Furtado had provided me with a new Toyota truck and José
Augusto's supervisor, Augusto Silva, to take me to Bafatà, the
largest town in the country of the Fula. The road had just been
paved by the Chinese. We passed a woman washing her breasts
at a public faucet, and a field of shimmering blue flowers.
Augusto Silva told me that there was no taboo against extramarital sex for the Fula women, as there was among the Manjaco,
and that there was no apparent correlation between AIDS and
circumcision, which like scarification is more common in the
rural areas where the disease is still rare. The Fula practice a
moderate form of circumcision. The operation is usually performed before the age of ten, Augusto Silva told me, so "it is
not a health problem because the tissue has healed long before
the girl starts having sex." He was more worried about another
practice of Fula, the levirate: when a man dies, his brother or
closest male relative inherits his wife. If the man died of AIDS,
there was a good chance his widow had the virus, too.

The hospital at Bafatà had a beautiful view. Tailors stitched
Muslim *boubous* at sewing machines in the streets below, and
a rolling pastoral landscape spread in the distance. We met
there with José Pedro Gonçalves, the regional director of public
health, and several doctors and nurses. Gonçalves told me that
there had been only one case of AIDS at the hospital, a thirty-
five-year-old typist for the police who had come from Bissau and
had since died there. Only one man out of a thousand adults in
the area who had been recently interviewed had confessed to
being a homosexual. Homosexuality, he said, was very taboo.
Most tribes in Equatorial Africa don't even seem to have a word
for homosexual. Gonçalves said that it was an insult to ask a

woman about anal intercourse, and that it was taboo for her to have sex when she was pregnant, because of a belief that the growing fetus would be harmed. Sex was also taboo for her during the two and a half years that she breastfed her child, because it was believed that her milk would be spoiled and her child would get diarrhea. Both taboos are widespread in Africa. Gonçalves thought that they encouraged the husband to "look elsewhere." We talked about the suspension in the urban populations of the taboo against sex during menstruation, which may be part of the reason why there is more AIDS in the city than in the country.

AT THE NATIONAL LABORATORY, on the edge of the city, I watched a technician named Mario José Gomes screen a batch of forty sera from a maternity ward and a transfusion center for HIV-2. He spun four cubic centimeters of blood to separate the lighter yellow serum from it, and he mixed ten microliters of serum with a milliliter of buffer; then he washed in PBS and distilled water a plaque he had prepared with antigen and left in the refrigerator for a day three times; then he poured the serum into two orifices. After leaving it for an hour and washing the plaque again he did something—by now I had lost him—with ten milliliters of buffer and ten microliters of alkaline phosphatase conjugated anti-human 1gC (Y-chain specific) produced in swine; and three equally complicated steps later, if I understood him correctly, he told me he would finally have the result. He showed me a batch of forty sera from the same source that he had screened earlier that morning. There were three positives, three slightly yellower orifices. The rest were clear. And this was the ELISA, the easier of the two antibody detection tests, a simple color reaction, an "enzyme-linked immuno-absorbent assay" that does not require sophisticated instruments like a spectrophotometer, unlike the Western Blot test that is used to confirm the ELISA positives and entails, as one scientific paper describes it, "radiommunprecipitation-sodium dodecyl-sulfate-polyacrylamide gel electrophoresis." There is desperate need in Africa for a simpler test that produces quick, reliable results.

NILS HOEJLYNG WAS involved in a Danish measles project that had been going on for eight years, tracing fifteen hundred family clusters in four of Bissau's *bairros*. He took me to the house of the widower of the first Guinean woman to be diagnosed with AIDS. The man's daughter came to the door. She said that he had died of "fever" in the Hospital Simão Mendes a month ago. The man had been second in charge of the fishing port, comparatively well off. "He would have had more than one wife," Hoejlyng said. "I don't know what the disease was that came to our house," the daughter said sadly. Hoejlyng said it was illegal to tell her. Her younger brother had also died, officially of hepatitis. "His blood was HIV negative, but he had the symptoms of AIDS—bleeding gums, anemia. He died of wasting." I asked if he could have been a false negative (false negatives are rarer than false positives, but they, too, occur, when tests designed for HIV-1 fail to pick up the presence of HIV-2 antibodies). Nils said, "What if he really was a negative? He will always be that officially." The daughter said, "I am the mother now of my four younger brothers and my own son. *E destino.* Life goes on." She was grieving but she managed a warm smile when we took our leave.

On Hoejlyng's wall there was a map of his *bairro* with a red pin stuck in each house where there had been a case of diarrhea from *Cryptosporidium*. *Cryptosporidium* is a protozoan, and one of the causes of diarrhea in many Western AIDS patients. I had seen it under a microscope in Lisbon—bright red, lethal, against a plain background of green fungus. Hoejlyng was testing a hypothesis that *Cryptosporidium* was the major parasitical cause of non-AIDS-related wasting in children. He had tested the blood and stool of every child under five in each house. Twenty percent of the houses had pins in them, and there was severe wasting in half of them. The fatality rate was seven to ten percent, even after treatment with rehydration salts. "This is a child killer, more than AIDS," he told me. The sera had been sent to Denmark for HIV-2 testing. Hoejlyng hadn't gotten the results, but he was expecting a positive in two to five percent of the households. "The promiscuity in this *bairro* is high," he said. "The men are Muslims. They average two and a half wives and they all say they have a lot of women on the side. There is a *criolo* expression, *mangare del' na caminha*. It means to fool around with women on the road. They all do it. I happen to know for a fact that my neighbor is positive. It's very annoying that I can't tell him. We're pulling out if we can't publish our results beyond the scientific community."

EIGHTY PERCENT OR so of the AIDS in Africa is transmitted sexually and so the sexual behavior of Africans is something that has to be understood if one is to make sense of the epidemic. Many Africans take exception to the term "promiscuous," just as they object to the word "prostitute." Perhaps a better term is the sociologist George Becker's "sex-positive." A sex-positive culture is one like that of the Mangaians of Polynesia, among whom sex for both men and women is a major recreational activity and abstinence is in fact thought to be physically harmful; a ready example of a sex-negative culture is Victorian England. By this definition, African, and tropical people in general, are unquestionably sex-positive. African men, whether they live in villages or cities, tend to be womanizers, and the women put up with it or participate in it depending on how much freedom they are allowed by their culture. The Fula are more promiscuous than the Manjaco, for example. But the greatest variation in sexual behavior is between the urban and rural populations. Urbanization has been a tremendous liberator of sexual activity. Such curbs as exist in the *tabancas* rapidly disintegrate in Bissau, particularly for the women.

One morning Furtado provided me with a car and a virile young driver, who seemed to be on intimate terms with all the pretty girls in town. They would wave to him from street corners as we passed. He was twenty-eight, married with four children, but "marriage here . . . is something else," as a European AIDS researcher told me. My driver picked up one of his paramours, a vivacious nurse, herself married, gave her a lift to where she was going, and as she was leaving, they set a rendezvous. I asked how many girlfriends he had. "For example, last Saturday I had two. One once, the other twice. I gave the first two thousand pesos, the second fifteen hundred. The more money you have, the more women you can get." This was not prostitution, he insisted. It was a present. It was customary to give the women something. Furtado agreed. "There is no prostitution in our country," he insisted. "Bissau is small enough that everybody knows everybody. A *mal creada* who had sex for money would bring shame on her family. They do it *por amizade*, out of friendship."

On Saturday night I checked out the Tropicana, the hottest night spot in Bissau. It was a pretty tame scene compared to the nightlife of Kinshasa or Nairobi, no single girls waiting to be picked up, just friends out for a good time, dancing disco rumbas and fast *pimpilhos*, their teeth and eyeballs phosphorescent purple in the strobe light. The taximan who took me back to the hotel drove me past one of the two *zonas*, or red-light districts. "The government discourages it, but it still goes on," he said. "Principally in this house." The shades were drawn, a dozen cars were parked outside. The *zona* was a Portuguese institution that had been introduced for the soldiers stationed there; prostitution doesn't exist in the *tabancas*. Furtado said the sexual *vagabundagem* in the capital was "an urban phenomenon. We are imitating your libertinage."

THE HOSPITAL Simão Mendes. Gamey zoo smell tinged with retch. Anterooms filled with forlorn, patient women. A typical large African hospital, not as bad as some, not as bad as the one in Mozambique where, because of civil war, there is sometimes no water or power for days, and "you go in with one disease and come out with three," as a doctor who worked there told me. I dashed through a morning deluge into the internal medicine ward where male AIDS patients were being treated by Dr. Bicose Jayme Nandaye, a gastroenterologist and member of the National Commission for the Struggle Against AIDS, which Furtado heads. The smell in the ward was different. It was of diarrhea, of stale sweat mingled with the stench of watery stool and gastric juices, a nauseating smell, the smell of death, of people shitting to death. Dr. Jayme said the smell was strong because many of the patients were from the country and had poor hygiene.

"Two we had died recently," he told me. "One was suspected of having AIDS. He had diarrhea and wasting, edema of the inferior members, and he was anemic. He came two days ago and died this morning. We didn't have time to test him for HIV. He was negative for TB." Dr. Jayme hung up an X-ray of the man's chest for me to see. "He probably had pneumonia, probably AIDS." The other, a thirty-four-year-old Fula, had died a few days earlier. We looked over his records. He had been questioned about his sexual habits. "They always admit to having had heterosexual vaginal sex, never to oral or anal sex." (This is the general attitude in sub-Saharan Africa. Oral sex is repugnant except to those who have been introduced to it by whites and learned to like it, anal sex "an abomination.") There were questions on travel history, transfusion, acupuncture, scarification, circumcision, pierced ears, medicinal bleeding, injections. It was a good questionnaire. The trouble was that it had been carelessly filled out.

I studied the records of another dozen apparent AIDS victims. They had only been given the ELISA test that revealed antibodies to HIV-2. The results had not been confirmed by Western Blot. The victims were coming from all over the country.

A Cuban nurse took me to patient Q. and explained that he was suffering from intense lack of air, wasting, anorexia, and had been having diarrhea for months. He was a bearded black stick figure, a wilted wraith on white sheets. I could have made a ring around his upper arm with my thumb and forefinger. The nurse said he was a worker in a cane distillery. He claimed (in her translation of his *criolo*) that he hadn't had sex in three years, wasn't married, and had no children. A *caipira*, Dr. Jayme said—a hick, a bumpkin who didn't know what had hit him. He kept looking at me with an expression of tearful, hurt, pleading, hopeless resentment, his eyes seeming to ask, "What is this? What did I do?"—for answers no one could—or would— give. At first he said he had never been out of the country or even to Bissau, though he had been born thirty kilometers from the capital. Later he said he had lived in Bissau about three years ago for "a long time" and had had many women there.

Patient A. gave his age as nineteen. His test result had not come back yet. Patient A., too, was clearly dying, but he seemed less fazed by his fate, almost cheerfully alert. He came

from the *tabanca* of Bisassima, a rural area in the south. He
had been having diarrhea for six months. He said he was single
and for the last six years had been driving a tractor around
Cantchungu. When he was seventeen he spent six years in
Bissau. But that would make him twenty-nine, I said. Further
questioning determined his age to be probably twenty-seven.
When he was here did he have many women? Yes, he said.
And also at the *tabanca*.

Out on the veranda, a crazy woman was singing in the rain.

"So WHAT ARE your impressions?" Furtado asked me. It was
our last meeting, and he had assembled several other members
of the National Commission for the Struggle Against AIDS in
his office. The records indicate that each month two or three
new patients in their last stages come to the hospital and die
within a week or two, I said. They seem to be coming from all
over the country, but most of them had a good time in Bissau
a few years back. There were two ways of interpreting this sparse,
scattered epidemiological pattern: Either HIV-2 was not usually
pathogenic, that is, disease-causing, and the patients who were
surfacing were just the unfortunate few afflicted ones, and their
numbers would more or less remain at this low level (this is
what Myron Essex, the American expert on HIV-2, and his
people at Harvard School of Public Health think), or—a more
disturbing possibility—HIV-2 has a longer incubation period
than HIV-1 and just hasn't started producing disease yet in all
the people who are infected with it. This is what Luc Montagnier
and his people at the Pasteur Institute in Paris think. In some
ways (I did not have the courage to say this, but a number of
epidemiologists have since agreed with me), the pattern looked
as if it could be the beginning of a massive epidemic, like water
coming to a boil.

KINSHASA

From Bissau I flew up to Dakar, the capital of Senegal, where AIDS doesn't seem to be much of a problem. The Islamic sanctions against adultery and premarital sex are more strictly observed here and are evidently a deterrent to the spread of the virus. Perhaps the male sex drive is better contained by the practice of polygamy than it is by the pretense of monogamy that the other countries make. "I have three wives," one Sénégalais told me, "*et ça suffit.*"

From Dakar I took a long flight down the Guinea Coast, which extends from Senegal to the Zaire (formerly the Congo) River. We made a stop in Abidjan, the capital of the Ivory Coast, which seems to be a transition zone for both the West African and the Central African viruses, HIV-2 and HIV-1. High levels of antibody response to both, sometimes in the same person, are reported—20 percent for HIV-2 in prostitutes, 5 percent in control groups; 19.8 percent for HIV-1 in prostitutes, 3.7 percent in control groups. In another study, 43 percent were HIV-1 positive, 5 to 15 percent for HIV-2, and 44 percent for both. Scientists at the Washington AIDS conference, a few months earlier, had talked about "double infection." Now they are more cautious, and are calling it "cross reactivity." (They haven't isolated both viruses in anyone, but blood samples have antibodies for both viruses.)

During the eight-hour flight I studied seroprevalence figures—the apparent HIV infection rates—for the countries we flew over. There are several problems with the statistics. Much of the data from Africa is based only on ELISA testing, so a large part of the dramatically high numbers that are being thrown out are false positives.

Alain Georges, the director of the Bangui branch of the Pasteur Institute, told me that the test gives a false positive rate of about twenty-five percent when a high-risk group (sexually promiscuous young adults, malnourished children, TB patients) is sampled. That is, a quarter of those who test positive in an ELISA test will come up negative when the Western Blot test is given. When the ELISA is given to the "general" population, about sixty-six percent of those who test positive will not be confirmed as positive by the Western Blot. The reason for this is not clear. It may have to do with the nutritional condition of the people tested, or it may be that high levels of infection with parasitic organisms like the malaria plasmodium "confuse" the test. Human error—the test has a number of complex steps, many opportunities to mess up—poor laboratory conditions (lab standardization and quality assurances are "just not possible" in Africa, an American AIDS diagnostician told me), lack of distilled water, not easy to come by, all will produce "sticky sera." Which means that much of the data on the level of infection in Africa is worthless.

Another problem is that the statistics are based on small, random samplings that may not represent the general population. The control groups are often hospital workers, who are more likely to be exposed to contaminated blood (it is often not screened at all) and take fewer precautions in general when handling patients than their Western counterparts do. They may also have special sexual characteristics of their own. These problems would tend to inflate the reported rates of infection. On the other hand, there are probably many carriers who are not being detected or reported. African governments are very sensitive and defensive about their AIDS problems. But then no statistically sound sero-survey has been conducted on the general population of any country, including the West.

IN THE EVENING, we finally touched down in Kinshasa, the swinging capital of Zaire. Zaire's reputation for being the "cradle of AIDS" rests on a shred of evidence: a serum collected in 1959 in Leopoldville, as Kinshasa was then called, and stored for many years in Seattle. It tests positive for HIV and is the earliest trace of the virus from anywhere. But a number of scientists are skeptical about it. "When you only have one specimen, you better be damn sure where it comes from," one of them told me.

The next positive serum dates from 1969 and, disconcertingly, comes from St. Louis, Missouri. Its discovery was a shocker, a piece of the puzzle that doesn't fit. The blood was from a dead fifteen-year-old black youth, Robert R. Doctors perplexed at his death had saved his blood and tissues for two decades. His autopsy had found small, purplish lesions of Kaposi's sarcoma, the rare cancer at that point found only in textbooks, elderly Austrian Jews and Italians, and in Central Africa, where it is endemic. Robert R. also had swollen lymph nodes in the neck, and the sexually transmitted disease, chlamydia. He had suffered severe weight loss before dying of pneumonia—a typical AIDS profile. Rectal lesions and chronic hemorrhoids suggest that he may have been homosexual.

The St. Louis serum throws a wrench into the African-origin theory. Why should HIV crop up in the blood of a St. Louis teenager in 1969, a decade before the disease began to strike other Americans? Robert Garry, a virologist at Tulane, one of the scientists working on the serum, told me the virus that killed Robert R. seems to have been "closely related to the strains now epidemic in the U.S." I asked if there were any major differences between the American, the European, and the African strains, and he said no. What was known about Robert R.? "By all accounts he never left the St. Louis area." I asked if Robert R.'s virus could have evolved in America. Why did it have to be African when there was no evidence it was? Why should Africa have a monopoly on immunosuppressive retroviruses? Garry said that it was "within the realm of possibility" that Robert R. had been infected with an endemic American virus, and that the African and the American AIDS epidemics were in fact "two parallel events" rather than one that had arisen out of the other. He said he was trying to isolate Robert R.'s virus, or at least parts of its genes, but it was hard isolating virus from tissues that had been frozen for so long. "There may have been HIV in Europe or here for hundreds of years," he told me. He sent me a recent article on the Euro-American origin of AIDS in the *Journal of the National Medical Association*. It reported that there had been sporadic cases of virulent Kaposi's sarcoma in young European and American men as far back as 1902, and speculated that some of them may have been caused by HIV.

"Something has to happen to make an endemic virus become an epidemic one," Garry told me. "Perhaps changes in the virus itself, perhaps sociocultural changes like the sexual revolution of the seventies that generated the AIDS epidemic in America and the urbanization and attendant rise in promiscuity that generated the epidemic in Africa. Both epidemics took off at more or less the same time." Other researchers use the term "amplification system." The gay revolution in the States and the urbanization of equatorial Africa provided "amplification systems" for the virus. "The question of where it started is important not only politically and historically, but scientifically," Garry went on. "It may help us understand what made the virus change from an endemic one to one that could be spread."

The next trace of AIDS, after Robert R., turns up in blood from pregnant women in Kinshasa collected in 1970. Zaire also provided one of the earliest cases of the strange new illness to come to the attention of Western doctors. By 1976 Grethe Rask, a Danish doctor who had come to work in Zaire in 1964, had been inexplicably weary for two years. She was losing weight, and her lymph glands were swollen. For the previous four years she had been in charge of a primitive hospital in Abumombazi, a remote village in northern Zaire, where there were no rubber gloves or disposable needles. Rask returned to Denmark, where she died on December 12, 1977, of a progressive lung disease of unknown etiology. An autopsy revealed that her lungs had been filled with a rare organism, *Pneumocystis carinii*, now recognized to be AIDS-related.

The oldest American case reported so far after Robert R. is that of an intravenous drug user in 1976. By then the virus was established on three continents, Africa, North America, and Europe. Now that whites were dying, the medical community was beginning to take notice. The first cases in Europe all tracked to Africa. But how could the disease have gotten to America, where by the late seventies (it became apparent later) it was firmly ensconced in the homosexual population on both coasts? One theory is that it came from Haiti. In the mid-sixties a large number of Haitians went to Zaire to fill middle-management positions in the newly independent state. They were sent back by President Mobutu in the early seventies, and it is possible that they took HIV with them. But the so-called "Haitian connection" doesn't seem to hold up. There were cases of AIDS in America before the first reported one in Haiti in 1978, and the sex ratio of the Haitian victims was at first overwhelmingly male—the Western pattern, not the African one. It seems more likely that poor Haitian men were selling themselves to vacationing Western gays, who infected them; later, as these men infected their wives and other women, the sex ratio became more equal, the epidemic heterosexual. When I asked Luc Montagnier about an Africa-to-Haiti-to-America route, he said, "Why couldn't it have been the other way around?" Many scientists ask the same question.

Another theory is that Cubans brought it back from Angola, which shares a long border with Zaire. In the late seventies the Cuban government purged the army of "undesirables," among whom were a number of homosexual veterans who had served in Angola, where Castro was supporting the new government of Agostinho Neto. Many of these men ended up in Miami, now one of the largest centers of AIDS in the U.S.

A third theory is the Peace Corps connection. During the early seventies the U.S. became very interested in Zaire for strategic reasons. It was a large new nation struggling to establish its political identity, wedged between two already leftist countries. So there was a massive infusion of Peace Corps volunteers and advisers from USAID and other agencies. A recent study of Danes returning from development projects in Africa found over eleven percent of them seropositive. The returning Peace Corps volunteers were never tested.

In any event, by 1983 "there was a suggestion of something happening in Zaire," recalls Thomas Quinn, an epidemiologist with the National Institute of Allergy and Infectious Diseases who had studied a homosexual disease known as gay bowel syndrome in Seattle and had been on the first team called in to assess the AIDS epidemic in Haiti. That year he was invited to help set up a research and surveillance project in Kinshasa called Projet SIDA. Ros Widy-Wirsky, a Polish epidemiologist who was then based in Kinshasa, and is now a consultant for Uganda's AIDS program, remembers the arrival of the Americans late in 1983. "I thought the American epidemiologists must have been hard up for work. They kept coming up with exotic things—legionnaire's disease, toxic shock syndrome. Now they were talking about this strange new immunodeficiency syndrome. I didn't believe them at first. Then we went into the internal medicine ward at Mama Yemo Hospital. They kept pointing to emaciated patients on the beds. 'There's one.' 'There's another.' 'Diarrhea, weight loss, cutaneous eruptions, pruritis, oral thrush—the classic symptoms. . . .' "

Quinn and his colleagues identified thirty-eight cases of AIDS at Mama Yemo right off the bat. The thing that struck them was the one-to-one sex ratio. In America there were seventeen male AIDS patients for every woman. "Here it was taking on the appearance of a heterosexual disease," Quinn recalled.

BEFORE I LEFT New York I had called the state department for traveler's advice. I said I was going to Kinshasa and asked if there was anything I ought to know about. "The main thing is to keep your pants on," the man at the Zaire desk said.

Kinshasa, with a population of roughly three million people, is the New York of Central Africa, a mecca of modernity. The place to stay there is the Intercontinental Hotel. L'Inter, as everyone calls it, is partly owned by President Mobutu, and his informers are said to be all over the place. A lot of stuff was going down around the pool when I went down for a dip the next morning. While stunning *citoyennes* and Vietnamese girls basked in the sun (it was the dry season here now), Brazilians cut illegal arms deals, American fly-boys eyed the scene through mirrored Ray-Bans. Now what are you guys doing here? I asked one. Oh, we're just doing some exercises at Kamina, an air base in the south, he said in an Arkansas drawl. He had been a mercenary here during Tshombe's unsuccessful bid to overthrow Mobutu. You couldn't be airlifting matériel to Savimbi now, could you? Who, us? he said with an ingenuous grin. Jonas Savimbi is the head of Unita, a guerrilla group trying to overthrow the government of Angola. The Soviets were combating the not-so-covert aid to Unita with a stunning disinformation campaign, claiming that the United States was spreading AIDS in southern Zaire as a biological warfare experiment.

Camille, an old friend from Kinshasa, joined me for a poolside lunch. After twenty years on its own, Zaire finally seemed to be stabilizing, he told me. The IMF had turned the money into real currency, and the black market and official rates were nearly the same. The *matabish*, or bribe, was still institutionalized, but the government seemed to be sincerely trying to crack down on corruption. The most encouraging thing, Camille said, was that Mobutu and his family and tribe had skimmed off all they needed. Mobutu's personal fortune was estimated at $5 billion. Now everybody wanted him to stay because his successor and his family and tribe would be starting at zero.

But what about the AIDS situation? I asked. How bad is it? It's not that obvious, he said. It was not as if they were dying in the streets, *comme des poulets*, as a man on the plane had told me. The average annual incidence of AIDS in Kinshasa between 1983 and 1985 was only 389 cases per million, according to Projet SIDA. Most Kinois didn't know any *atteints* personally. "I think it must be a *maladie imaginaire* because I don't know anyone who has it," a waitress at L'Inter had told me. Indeed there was a joke in Kinshasa that SIDA stands for *Syndrome Imaginaire pour Décourager les Amoureux*. Compared to the pleasures at hand, AIDS seemed a remote, farfetched castigation. The only behavioral change that Camille had noticed was that after a Western-influenced run on slim *citoyennes*, hefty women were back in vogue, because they were thought less likely to have the wasting syndrome.

The government of Zaire had been up and down on its position vis-à-vis foreign journalists. At an AIDS conference in Washington a few months earlier I had met Matondo Massamba, the convivial number-two man for the department of public health, and we had drafted a delicately phrased letter to the ministry explaining that I wanted to do an "objective study of infectious diseases" in Zaire. I had sent it off several months ago and had heard nothing since. When I presented myself at Massamba's office he said that my letter was still with *sécurité*. "It could be there for months." He advised me to just proceed cautiously and find out what I could. "*Il faut être très prudent.* Don't go to the university. They will arrest you."

My journalist colleagues had not exactly paved the way for me. An American television camera crew had supposedly forged papers authorizing them to film the AIDS patients in Mama Yemo Hospital. Then there had been an uproar in the French press about Dr. Zirimwabago Lurhuma's human experiments with the AIDS vaccine he was working on. *Essais sauvages,* the experiments were called. Lurhuma was working on both a preventive and an interventive vaccine, and the Zaïrois were very proud of him. The criticisms were regarded as a "racist campaign of denigration."

AIDS in Zaire is almost entirely urban, Massamba told me, and "If we act quickly we can keep it from spreading to the rest of the people." He attributed the epidemic to promiscuity. "The independent tribal mentalities have merged, and we have a *crise morale,*" he explained. "Our youth has become too emancipated, loose *dans leur moeurs.* Provocative advertisements and music are having a bad influence. It is the twenty-to-forty-year-olds who are the SIDA people. Suddenly they are in an urban culture, away from family constraints." Some studies support Massamba's theory that the incidence of infection in rural areas was low and not increasing, but others have found alarmingly high rates in the bush. Typically, numbers can be produced to support both views.

Massamba was worried about the increase in diseases other than AIDS. Since independence, he told me, many diseases that had been more or less under control had been coming back, although some of the across-the-board rise in reported illness was probably due to advances in diagnostic methods. There had been a big cholera epidemic in 1977. A lot of children in eastern Zaire were dying in an outbreak of shigellosis when I was there in 1981. "Tuberculosis is back in force, leprosy, sleeping sickness, bilharziasis, onchocerciasis [African river blindness, mainly in the southern region of Kasai], congenital abnormalities due to first-trimester malnutrition, goiters leading to cretinism, mental retardation, repeated abortion, and infant mortality—there has been a recrudescence of these endemic diseases in the interior." Why? "Because of bad habits, socioeconomic conditions, lack of medicine. Before independence the health situation was much better," he said. When the Belgians pulled out in 1960, the entire modern infrastructure, which was quite impressive—roads, hospitals, schools, agricultural production, postal service, etc.—collapsed. There still hasn't been a new hospital in Kinshasa, for instance, since independence, when the city's population was only 300,000.

Thomas Quinn saw the breakdown of health services in Africa during the seventies as one of the catalysts of the epidemic. Brooke Schoepf, an American medical anthropologist working with an AIDS education program in Kinshasa, agreed. The current global economic crisis has had severe repercussions on health budgets in Africa and a terrible impact on the collective immune system, she said. When the IMF made budget tightening a condition for giving new loans and rescheduling payments on existing ones, health and agriculture were the first to suffer. "The budgets were already stringent," Schoepf said. "Now they're even [tighter]. So that takes care of health and nutrition, doesn't it?"

Massamba had said he would take me that night to the zone of Matonge, the throbbing heart of what a tourist brochure at L'Inter described as Kinshasa's "captivating nightlife." I waited an hour but he didn't show, so I took off for Matonge with a taximan named Dieudonné. The zone was full of dives, juke joints, open-air dancing bars known as *ngandas*, with names like Harlem Dancing Club, Dolly Club, New York Disco Dancing, Un Deux Trois. Dieudonné used an expression that captured the Zaïrois vision of the dolce vita, "Rumba, Ndumba, and Primus." Rumba is the intoxicating music, Primus is the heady beer—a bottle or two will loosen up anybody. A *ndumba* is an unmarried girl in Lingala, the language of Bas Zaire, a *femme libre* in French. It can be used pejoratively to mean a whore.

And there was a new word, Dieudonné told me, "Sidanie," which is a girl's name that puns on SIDA.

According to Brooke Schoepf, the *femmes libres* are primarily those who took part in the postindependence and ongoing rural exodus. "The colonial power kept the women out of town and broke up the families because it didn't want to pay a family wage," she explains. "The women had to stay and work in the fields to feed the colonial labor force. There was tremendous displacement and social disruption. After independence many women escaped to the towns because the drudgery of forced cultivation was so unbearable and became second or third wives or *femmes libres*." And even after the men came home to the villages, it was the women who continued to do most of the work, the digging, the hauling of water and firewood. That is the way it has always been in Africa. So it is not surprising that the women would want to break away, that as traditional mores were relaxed, there was an increase in divorce, and once they were in the city, perhaps with several children to feed, away from their extended family where there was always someone to help them out, the only way they could survive was by selling themselves. "The women need to make love more than the men do," Dieudonné explained. "They need to make love to eat. Here if you make love to a woman you must pay her. Some are *deuxième bureaux*, unofficial second wives, some are *deuxième bureaux laissés*, mistresses who have been let go. Many are students *sans soutien*. They lack work and educational opportunities in their region. They have no other way of surviving. But they all make love with feeling."

Dieudonné and I checked out the Hotel Matonge, where there was supposed to be a lot of action, but it was only eight o'clock. Too early. The men had finished work and were still at the soccer game. They hadn't hit the bars yet. The girls had not yet begun to appear. So we killed an hour over bottles of

Primus. As we drained our glasses Dieudonné became gloomy. "I think about *la vie actuelle*. *Il y'a trop de femmes, trop de problèmes*. There are many products for the woman to rub on, cosmetics for them to apply. She can't read and sometimes the products are *jetés* and reused and give her sickness. Expired medicine, old antibiotics, *syringes jetés* are being sold in the pharmacies and in the market. Now there are no products *pour les moustiques* and everybody has fever. Before independence there was a plane and a truck and men with pumps to spray against the mosquitoes. I am worried also about *maladies* from the cadavers. They used to be buried two or three meters deep far from town. Now they are being buried in town, only fifty centimeters deep, and without *médicaments*."

Dieudonné had the apocalyptic vision of many Third World philosophers. He believed that the curtain was falling, that the Flood was coming. If this was indeed what was happening, we in America were still insulated from it, unaware that the water was rising. We were a Cadillac and the countries of Africa were beat-up jalopies ready to throw a rod. As we glided serenely down the highway, we rarely met with the sudden accidents, the rude raw intrusions of reality that were daily occurrences in most of the world. Only rarely did the concrete section of a bridge collapse, plunging us into the rain-swollen river. But it was already eminently clear that the old ways in Africa were no good anymore. Millions were leaving the villages and heading for the cities, where there was nothing for them, no work, only perdition. And AIDS was the last straw, the final flail. It played right into the gathering millenarian terror.

By nine-thirty the men were in the bars, waiting for *l'arrivée des femmes*. The women came by eleven. In his booth the *animateur* put on a mellow rumba. Couples took to the floor and began to dance slow and loose, shaking their shoulders and flapping their elbows deliciously, the women's hands moving suggestively, almost cupping their breasts. It was like the old erotic tribal dances. Nobody seemed to have gotten the word that the party was over, that for many this was a dance of death. We sat in an outdoor *ndonga* with two sisters and a man. The older sister, Agnes, was twenty, the younger, Doroté, was an innocent sixteen-year-old, a child who had come up a year ago from a town in Bas Zaire to go to school. She was shyly lip-synching the words of a mellow rumba love song.

Doroté had hooked up with a thirty-seven-year-old gynecologist from Nairobi, although they had no language in common. Soon Agnes went off with a chauffeur from one of the foreign embassies. "She will get a thousand to three thousand zaires [ten to thirty dollars] depending on the man's love," Dieudonné said. "She is more experienced, and she supports the younger one, but she is already used. Now it is the *petite soeur* that the men of all ages will want to take advantage of."

FORTY PERCENT OF the people in Africa are in their sexually active years, more than anywhere else in the world. There is great concern that the young movers and shakers, the middle-management cadres and bureaucrats, the educated elite painfully built up from nothing over the last twenty years, will be especially hard hit by AIDS because it is they who can best afford to run around with many women, and having many women is a status symbol, part of the image of the successful African male.

A study by the Harvard Institute of Development has tried to assess the economic impact of illness and premature death due to AIDS in the Third World; the product loss from incremental mortality among working-age adults in the mining, transport, and urban-elite sectors, and how much money will have to be diverted from household and national incomes to take care of patients. The study estimates that in Zaire by 1994 the disease will cost $350 million a year, that there will be an eight-percent product loss over the 1984 productivity figure due to the premature death of working-age adults. This is more than the total foreign aid Zaire receives (though peanuts compared to the estimated cost of AIDS for the U.S. by then: $292 billion). The projected cost for seven other sub-Saharan countries, $980 million, will exceed overseas development assistance from all sources.

In 1986, the thirty-year-old married son of Zambian president Kenneth Kaunda died of AIDS, but it is unclear how many similar cases there were. Ngaly Bosenge, the director of the newly formed Bureau de Coordination Central de la Commission Nationale de la Lutte Contre le SIDA, did not believe that the elite was being particularly hard hit. "The cadres can support a *deuxième bureau*," he told me. "Most of the men who go to the *femmes libres* are from the lower class. They go when they get a little money. It represents a moral satisfaction to take out a girl wearing gold and jewelry. The cadres go to the *boîtes* to dance with their *deuxième bureaux*, not to find a prostitute." Projet SIDA has found no socioeconomic gradation of seropositivity. Rich, poor, middle class seem to be equally infected in Kinshasa. But studies in Bangui and Nairobi have found lower-class, cheaper prostitutes with more contacts more likely to be infected. And in New York the great majority of AIDS cases are among inner-city blacks and Hispanics.

"You will find chasers of skirts, *le banditisme et la musique*, and serious people in Zaire as well," Ngaly went on. "The church is very strong." Fifty percent of the population is Catholic, twenty percent is Kimbanguist, ten percent other syncretic sects, and nearly three hundred Protestant groups have followings in the country. There are no figures for how many Zaïrois are devout Christians, but some estimate one-third. Christianity with its insistence on lifelong fidelity is a strong ally in the *lutte contre le SIDA*, in getting across the message that sex is not something to be engaged in lightly. Many churchgoing Kinshasans see the disease as a plague sent by God.

One afternoon I took in a charismatic born-again Catholic revival service at Notre Dame de Fatima, not far from L'Inter. The church was packed and overflowing with hundreds of people swaying and clapping in complex cross-rhythms as they sang their praise together. In their swelling devotionals, punctuated with the slapping of tambourines and the occasional ululating *cri de joie* of an oversouling woman, I seemed to hear the soul of Africa, and it was not hard to believe that there was a force greater than ourselves that had the answer; we certainly didn't, as far as SIDA was concerned.

"EDUCATION IS THE only vaccine we have for SIDA," a doctor in Kinshasa told me. "It is education, as H. G. Wells said, or catastrophe." There was a lot of talk about SIDA on Zairian television and lively debate on strategies of prevention and control in the Kinshasa papers. An article in *Elima* reported an effort by a street-theater troupe at *sensibilization sur le SIDA au moyen des marionettes*. The puppets performed in four compartments. In the first were *les malades*, defecating and covered with sores. The second showed the degree to which the scourge has alarmed the world, the Pope in the Vatican saying a mass for the victims of the horrible disease. Below, "savants and healers are searching for ways and means to find a vaccine or preferably a medicine to check this disease that haunts the human race." In the last compartment the *grand maître* Luambo Makini was in a recording studio singing his hit single, "Attention Na SIDA," the most important educational initiative in the *lutte*. Luambo is the Pan-African superstar rumba singer better known as Franco, the second most important figure in the country after Mobutu. I had picked up a cassette with Franco's song at the airport in Togo, and had been listening to it. It was a heavy rap, a song sermon that went on for ten minutes or so and spelled out the problem in detail. Stanzas in French alternated with ones in Lingala. Each verse was spoken against an insistent, seductive rumba phrase, rocking back and forth from the dominant to the subdominant, laid down by Franco's famous band, O.K. Jazz. "*O le SIDA est une terrible maladie,* / *Une maladie qui ne pardonne pas* / that spares nobody / SIDA ravages all the people / Recently Europe and the United States / have been accusing Africa of being / the cradle of SIDA / Asia was saying that it was untouched by the evil of SIDA / But today all the continents / Find that they are attacked . . . / The entire course of the society is victim, / Babies, children, young people, adults, old people / Workers, bureaucrats, cadres / men, women / Pastors, rabbis, imams, priests / And even the doctors, they too are vulnerable / SIDA can strike anyone / SIDA can kill / If everyone doesn't make an effort to protect himself. . . ."

CIRCUMSPECTLY, AS MATONDO Massamba (who said he had provided Franco with information about the high-risk activities) had advised, I went to Mama Yemo Hospital. Not wanting to jeopardize my mission with a run-in with *la sécurité*, who were all over the place with walkie-talkies, and having already seen patients wasting away at the Hospital Simão Mendes, I steered clear of the SIDA pavilion. A young Brazilian I met at L'Inter told me he had been curious to see the patients and had just walked into the pavilion one afternoon. "Everything was so disorganized I had no problem," he told me. "I went in with a perfumed handkerchief over my nose and mouth. There were no beds. The patients were lying on foam mattresses, four or five to a room. Lying in their own shit. What a way to die. I'm going back to Brazil. There is too much misery here."

Doctor X had seen many patients at life's edge in the SIDA pavilion. Some had cryptococcal meningitis, which knocks out vital motor functions and was responsible for an outbreak of dementia that took off with the *dépistage* of SIDA in Kinshasa during the eighties. Most were emaciated with diarrhea, "but that's not what kills them in the end," Dr. X told me. "They die of what we call 'the dwindles.' They just sort of smolder away."

Dr. X told me of a study at Projet SIDA in which a group of asymptomatic positives were being tracked over a period of time to see how many projected from ARC (AIDS-related complex) to AIDS. The pattern was no different from that of a cohort of gays that had been tracked in San Francisco: ten percent were projecting into ARC, six percent into AIDS. To him this meant that the "infectious disease burden" that Africans carry does not play a role. It didn't seem to have occurred to him to think about this in another way: that the Western gays who participated in *la ronde* of bar sex and incredible promiscuity in the seventies were in fact suffering from an infectious disease burden very similar to Africans'.

"But the time frame from AIDS to death is shorter here," Dr. X went on. "A San Francisco gay gets treated. Here there are limited resources." There is no way the average African could afford a drug like AZT, even if it were available. A year's worth costs more than ten thousand dollars.

Dr. X and I talked about the many candidates that have been proposed as cofactors by those who don't believe that HIV is the sole cause of AIDS. The intestinal-parasite cofactor theory is based on the fact that Africans, Haitians, and gays are all riddled with amoebas, *Giardia*, *Salmonella*, etc. Thomas Quinn had told me that the theory is not being considered seriously ("the parasites relate to killing people, but not to making them more susceptible," he said), but others believe that it bears looking into. The British genetic predisposition theory argues that one white blood cell group is more sensitive to HIV infection and is more common among Africans. It elicited a storm of letters in the British medical journal *The Lancet* and seems to have been effectively shot down. Some say that malaria makes you more susceptible to HIV infection, others say the opposite; a hard case for either has yet to be made. A number of other viruses have been proposed as cofactors: African swine virus, Epstein-Barr virus. Perhaps HIV opens the door to some yet unknown agent, like the unnamed virus reported to cause immune-system breakdown by Dr. Shyh-Ching Lo at the Armed Forces Institute of Pathology, in Washington. Perhaps Hepatitis B is a cofactor. HBV, which like HIV is transmitted by sex and blood, infects about ninety-five percent of the people in Africa after the age of thirteen and is eliminated by all but twenty-five percent of them. It was a big problem for gays during the sexual revolution. There is a theory that serum from the Third World for the Hepatitis B vaccine could have contained HIV and thus spread into the gay population, but Robin Ryder, the director of Projet SIDA, who worked previously on HBV-related liver cancers in Gabon, told me this was impossible because any HIV in the serum would have been killed three times during the preparation of the vaccine. "HIV lives only in special lymphocytes," he told me. "It's very heat-labile. If you put it on a table it dies."

Dr. X said that it was important to distinguish between two types of cofactors, those that accelerate the progress of the disease, that affect its natural history, and those that facilitate infection. There is only firm evidence for the second type: prostitute studies in Nairobi have shown that a history of sexually transmitted disease and genital ulcers caused by such STDs as chancres facilitate infection. The ulcers provide more host cells for the virus to latch on to and more infected cells for the partner to be exposed to. They also provide a portal of entry for the virus. "The ulcer is a portal," Dr. X went on. "You can pour HIV on your skin all day long and if there isn't a break in it nothing will happen." (This doesn't seem to be quite accurate. New evidence that HIV can directly infect cells of healthy tissue in the rectum and the vagina seems to indicate that tears or sores aren't necessary for transmission, although of course they make it more likely.)

We talked about the risk of being infected by a single sexual contact with an infected person. Estimates range from one in ten to one in a thousand. There are no believable figures, but it would seem that the virus is not very easily acquired when both partners are healthy. It is more readily transmitted to the woman, which would suggest that Zaïrois men are more promiscuous than women if the sex ratio of AIDS cases is equal.

He explained that heterosexual sex was a lot more risky and efficient as a mode of transmission in Africa than it is in the West because the levels of seropositivity are much higher and a lot more people have other diseases. I wondered if the way sex is performed has anything to do with it. For most Africans, sex is a matter of vigorous old-fashioned humping, often without foreplay, which means that there is insufficient lubrication, and the genitalia of both partners are therefore liable to abrasion. Some researchers have speculated that the duration of the sex act, and the *frottement*, or grinding, that the women of certain tribes are famous for, certain techniques like the *titikisha*, Swahili milling movement, and the *okuweta ekiwoto*, the frenzied twisting of the waistline of Baganda women, may play a role. In other tribes, like the Tutsi and the Kikuyu, the woman is not supposed to move during intercourse lest she be thought of as a prostitute. It seems reasonable that the longer the genitals are in contact and the more fluid that is emitted and the more *frottement* the greater the chance for infection. But like the theories about ritual scarification, female circumcision, and blood brotherhood, this is not supported by any scientific study.

IN THE MAMA Yemo complex there is one building given over to Projet SIDA. The atmosphere is completely un-African, one of air-conditioned American efficiency, permeated with a sense of urgency, people coming in and out all the time—nuns, security guards in jump suits stenciled AMERICAN EMBASSY, lab technicians with racks of blood samples corked in test tubes, a woman from the CDC doing placental studies—everybody putting in long hours, making every second count, no lunch breaks in this operation. The tone is set by Robin Ryder, a fit young man in his thirties who projects a let's-get-to-work and lick this sonofabitch attitude. Matondo Massamba gives him high marks: *"Il s'est adapté, et il est un bon formeur des jeunes chercheurs."* In Washington he had told me a little bit about Projet SIDA, about the cross-sectional studies they were working on, how they were studying a hundred consecutive blood donors, a hundred prostitutes in Kinshasa, a hundred patients at Mama Yemo, and coming up with a general seroprevalence estimate of eight percent (since revised down to five percent).

Ryder told me about his discordant-partner study (as one would expect, the longer they've been having sex, the more likely the infected one is to seroconvert, to start testing positive) and his condom-intervention studies. "Condoms have been a failure in family planning, but they failed because everybody wants a lot of kids. When you distribute condoms as a way of not dying it may be a different ball game," he said.

"If you're interested in preventing the spread of HIV, prostitutes are the group to start with," Ryder told me. "Educate, scare, motivate them. Organize *carnets de santé*, but that is going to be very hard to get together. A lot of men go to prostitutes casually. They are the hot point. In the U.S. the risk groups are

easily identified: gays, i.v. drug users, prostitutes, hemophiliacs. If you work on them you can eliminate ninety percent of the
cases. But here you sit on the National AIDS Committee and you
realize there is no high-risk group. The high-risk group is everybody between fifteen and forty-five. The whole damn population.
Sex is a big part of Africa. Take it away and there is nothing."

NAIROBI

The Ethiopian Airlines plane was due in Kinshasa at two in the
morning but it was two hours late. Then at last we were in the air,
headed for Nairobi, where I would connect with a flight to Kampala. In a few hours we were flying over the Western Rift Valley,
which is filled with lakes and vast herds of animals and recalls
the first chapter of Genesis. The valley is one of the epicenters of
speculation about the source of AIDS. There is a theory that ra-
dioactivity from the volcanoes on the valley's west flank caused
the mutation of the virus. There is also a theory, equally off the
wall, that the virus came in a meteor from outer space.

We reached Nairobi just in time to miss my connecting
flight to Kampala, and I found myself an unscheduled weekend
guest at the Hotel Ambassador, in the center of town. The
ambience here was very different from that of French or Portuguese Africa. This was the British colonial overlay: tea, queues,
schoolgirls in uniform, a residual atmosphere of intolerance
giving rise to a more developed black consciousness. The city
is very modern and European, a lot like Johannesburg, and it
was crawling with Americans in safari jackets. I went to the
movies: *Psycho III* or maybe *IV*. At 2 a.m. rowdies in the street
below my room started up the same ululating cries I had heard
in the church in Kinshasa, but here they were not *cris de joie*.
They sounded like shrieks of madness and alienation.

In the morning I took a taxi to Nairobi National Park, just

outside of town. The driver, a Kikuyu named Simon, had never looked through binoculars before, and he was knocked out. Giraffes, ostriches, zebra, bok were grazing in the tall grass with skyscrapers in the distance. We got talking about the dread disease. "It's funny how they always say it's us," Simon said. "First it's the African killer bees. Now it's AIDS."

We drove down to a little river lined with gallery forest, parked, and started walking. After a few hundred yards we met a wart hog with a big ugly head and nasty tusks, in the middle of the path. He stood his ground and stared us down for a few minutes, then moseyed off. We continued to a pool in which submerged hippos were occasionally surfacing to breathe under overhanging foliage. On the opposite bank a regal Masai woman had come down from her village to fill some plastic jerry cans. The river divided our two worlds.

I asked Simon to ask her in Swahili if she had heard of AIDS. She had, but knew no one, man or woman, with any kind of disease like this. She heard about it on the radio, that AIDS was in Kenya. She didn't know where it was but she was sure it was in the city. She understood that to prevent the disease, never shake hands with somebody.

On the way back to the car we spotted several green monkeys—the harborers of numerous viruses and the alleged natural reservoir of HIV—scrounging in an overturned garbage can. They were olive green, with grayish paws, white masks, and black muzzles, and less than two feet tall. I asked a ranger sitting under a nearby acacia tree if the monkeys were eaten. "In Kenya we don't eat monkeys," he told me. "Primates are just like humans, you know."

Whether the ancestor of HIV passed from monkeys to humans, and if so whether the transmission was a single, isolated event or occurred repeatedly, are two of the many unanswered questions about AIDS. Green monkeys are found throughout the

African AIDS belt, where they live in close contact with humans, raiding plantations, sneaking into back yards, being raised as pets, and in many places, if not in Greater Nairobi, being killed and eaten. Ingestion is unlikely as the mode of transmission, however, because the virus is unstable and is quickly killed by heat. A recent sampling of the blood of Pygmies in the Central African Republic, who have been eating monkeys for centuries, turned up no HIV. An accident while butchering a monkey, or blood from a monkey seeping into someone's cut, is a more likely mode.

Green monkeys can be vicious when cornered, but biting is not an efficient mode of transmission, since there isn't much virus in saliva. There are no documented cases of one human infecting another with HIV by biting, although several lawsuits are pending in the U.S. (a prostitute in Manhattan who bit a police officer trying to arrest her was charged with assault with a deadly weapon), and Luc Montagnier told me that a report of a pet store owner in Paris being infected by one of his monkeys may be published soon. The idea that the virus may have been transmitted by sexual contact with monkeys, which seems to have caught the fancy of some, is highly unlikely. Bestiality is not unknown in Africa, but it is rare. And anyway, green monkeys are much too small even for a pedophile. They are no bigger than groundhogs.

Several months ago a letter to *The Lancet* caused quite a stir. The correspondent reported a curious tribal practice on the island of Idjwi, in Lake Kivu, in the Western Rift Valley, that he had read about in a book on the sexual mores of Great Lakes Africans by a Zairian anthropologist named A. Kashamura. "To stimulate a man or a woman and induce them to intense sexual activity monkey blood was directly inoculated in the pubic area and also in the thigh and back," the letter reported. It did not say what kind of monkey blood was injected or what type of instrument was used for injection. And in any case, HIV levels on Idjwi are no higher than anywhere else in Central Africa.

That night Simon took me to Buffalo Bill's Saloon and Eating House. We sat at a table under a canvas wagon cover with a lantern hanging from its frame. I bought a round of beer for two girls from Uganda. Winifred was twenty, laughing and joking, but there seemed to be a desperation in her gaiety. She had left Uganda for "a change of life." Kenya was full of Ugandan girls who have crossed over the border to escape the civil chaos.

"I've never seen anybody with AIDS, so it takes a hard time to believe," she told me. "It's a sickness which you can't know. If you have flu, you sneeze, but this is a disease whereby you can't know." She paused thoughtfully, and went on. "AIDS is like an accident. You can't stop traveling in a vehicle if you have seen an accident. You can't stop moving. The same with AIDS. You can't stop living. We are together, I don't know if you have it. I'm just looking for a steady man to take care of me. You can get a steady man even in the world of streetwalking. But if you don't move how will a man see you?" I asked if she used "socks," the Ugandan term for condoms. She said yes, Urex, when she could get them, but "men pay more not to use them."

The whole AIDS question is very sensitive in Kenya. The government had been denying the existence of the disease for fear of its impact on tourism, then denying that it had been denying it. There had been some decline in the number of German sex tourists, probably because of bad press. According to a German magazine AIDS was introduced to Africa by American sailors on shore leave in Mombasa. There are wild stories about these sailors, how they come to Mombasa once a year and have certain injections for sexual vigor and can stay excited for twenty-four hours.

I had thought of hiring a Land-Rover and driving overland from Nairobi to Kampala, about four hundred miles northwest across Kenya and then around the northern rim of Lake Victoria. But the road was not clear, there were "thugs," as the Ugandan press called the various guerrilla groups along the border. Most of the trouble was in northern Uganda, with Obote's followers, the Acholi; Milton Obote had been president before Idi Amin and again after him, and a year ago had been thrown out by Yoweri Museveni. Museveni now had six rebel groups on his hands. One group calling itself the Holy Spirit Movement was led by a charismatic priestess, Alice Lakwena, who promised her followers that they would be immune from enemy bullets if they smeared magic oil on their bodies. Two thousand Ugandans had fled into Kenya to escape the fighting.

Uganda ranks with Guinea-Bissau as one of the world's ten least-developed countries. It has been ravaged by one civil war after another for the last two decades, and before that by inter-tribal conflict for centuries. It is one of the world's chronically unsettled spots, like Northern Ireland or the Middle East, and now it is being devastated by AIDS. The Lord is not smiling on these people.

Tensions had also been building between Kenya and Uganda, longstanding uneasy neighbors. Kenya had cut off direct-dial telephone communications to Uganda, and Uganda was retaliating by cutting off the electric power it provided to Kenya.

I was better off flying.

ENTEBBE AIRPORT, FAMOUS for the 1976 rescue of hostages by Israeli commandos. "If was not for war this country was very beautiful," my taxi driver tells me as we drove twenty miles from the airport to Kampala. The lush green hills of the rumpled plateau fall off to vast horizonless Lake Victoria. Entebbe is smack on the equator, but the four-thousand-foot elevation mitigates the heat and humidity. The temperature hovers at seventy, and it rains hard every other day.

Roadblock. Everybody out. Routine check for weapons or

anything out of the ordinary. Barefoot teenage soldiers in motley uniform unzip my duffel bag and spread its contents out on the grass. A fifteen-year-old with a machine gun flips through my up-side-down passport and passes it back. Onward. We pull over for a high-speed motorcade, a limo wedged among the motorcycles. "Big boss from out," my driver says. The ambassador of Norway. We reach Kampala, a once-splendid city now in decay, with a smattering of high rises, some of them abandoned in midconstruction and already reclaimed by the black fungus partial to concrete in the tropics. Huge, gangly marabou storks perch on eaves and rooftops like inscrutable gargoyles. The place looks as if the modern world washed in and washed out some time ago, leaving it high and dry. There is a curious bobbing, weaving pattern to the traffic flow as the cars and trucks avoid potholes.

Half the Speke Hotel, once a gracious colonial establishment, is now a charred black ruin, gutted by a mysterious fire a month ago, but one wing still stands, and there is a room in it for me. I settle in and go down to the veranda for a beer.

May I join you? A bearded white man is standing over me. Sure. Pull up a chair. His name is Sergei. A plastic and maxillofacial surgeon from Moscow, he has been working for a year at the Mulago Hospital. Most of his operations are for gunshot trauma and jaws broken by rifle butts. I tell him what I am doing here. "You can learn a lot about SPID here and you can get it too," he says. SPID is the Russian acronym for AIDS. Sergei tells me a joke about how AIDS stands for Amerikanskii Imperialisticheskii Dozhobnii Siphilis, Imperialistic American Rear-End Syphilis. The waiter brings a check for an incredible sum. It isn't that he is trying to cheat me but that he can't add. I send him back to redo the figures.

Dusk is falling. Hundreds of birds with curved wings and blunt bodies—nighthawks of some kind—are swooping in the bloodshot sky. I go up to my room and crash. In the wee hours there are sporadic bursts of gunfire right under my window.

In the morning I hear several theories about what it was all about. 1) Just bored soldiers shooting off their guns. 2) Guards shooting at thieves trying to hold up the Bat Valley Bar and Restaurant. 3) Soldiers shooting thieves with whom they were in cahoots for not turning over their cut of the take. This last is the correct theory. Three bodies are laid out in the roundabout next to the Speke.

I ask two men on the street if they can point me to the ministry of information, where I have to present myself for a foreign press card. The two men unhesitatingly point in opposite directions. The Third World information problem in a nutshell.

A few hours later, two young women in the ministry of health's public relations section take me down to the headquarters of the National AIDS Control Programme in Entebbe, past the botanical garden, out on a point sloping down to the lake. Nice spot here, I say. Tis cool on the lake except tis shining, one says. Beautiful country, I say. Tis ever green, the other says. I meet Ros Widy-Wirski, the program's chief epidemiologist, an irascible, warm-hearted Pole in his forties.

Like Robin Ryder, Widy-Wirski is working twelve hours a day, six to seven days a week, and not stopping for lunch. He was supposed to have been here only two months as a consultant with the World Health Organization to help set up the program, and he's already been here six. He isn't much interested in talking to me about the theory that the border of Uganda and Tanzania, along Lake Victoria, could be the endemic center of the disease. He isn't interested in historical questions.

In the next room I meet the head of the program, Dr. Samuel I. Okware, a suave, elegant man of about forty in a pinstriped suit. Okware is a veteran of international meetings, fluent in the ways of the West, with a master's in public health from the University of Minnesota. On a wall in his office is a poster that says "Love Carefully!" Framed in a heart is a lyre-horned Ankole steer tethered to a stake and under the heart the words, "Zero Grazing

Is the Answer." Zero grazing is a veterinary term, Okware tells me, "an agricultural metaphor which I have brought in to explain sex. Sex is hard to explain in Uganda without raising hairs. The term refers to the way you feed your animal in winter. You put him in a corral and feed him in one place. In Africa you tie the cow to a pole so that he eats within a locus, grazes within a circle, and can't reach the other attractive grass. It is the opposite of free-range grazing. I wanted something that was catchy and funny, to make a joke so people could bear it. AIDS is such a sad thing."

I ask about the big ethical question throughout Africa, that no one is telling the carriers that they have the virus, so they go on infecting others. "We don't tell the carrier because what will we do with him?" Okware says. "Plus he may be a false positive and one or two have committed suicide."

Uganda is the only African country to have officially adopted an open policy about AIDS. As a result of the openness, "world attention has focused on Uganda, but it is not the focal point of infection in Africa," Okware said. "Uganda is not special, it's not worse here. The numbers are higher because no one is looking elsewhere."

A few months ago a pair of reporters from *Reader's Digest* passed through and reported that "whole villages in the south are being decimated." The government hadn't liked that. Nor had the government liked what Dr. Wilson Carswell, a British surgeon and longtime resident of Uganda who had done much of the blood screening that gave the first indications of the gravity of the epidemic, told a stringer from the Manchester *Guardian*: "In ten years you won't have any trouble finding a parking space." Carswell had been expelled from the country, and now the government's policy wasn't so open.

THE LAB AT St. Francis General and Maternity Hospital was less well equipped than the typical science lab at an English secondary school. Late in 1985, when cases of AIDS began to appear at the hospital, a heroic woman named Sister Nelezinho Carvalho became worried that the blood supply could be contaminated and went to London to be trained in screening techniques. She returned with a Compact 2000 electronic blood test analysis machine and started testing. Fourteen percent of the blood proved to be infected. For months her machine was the only one in Kampala, and she and her assistant handled the blood samples and washed the test tubes without gloves and without bleach because neither was available. They knew the risk and accepted it. At least there would be safe blood for the patients having babies or an operation.

Sister Nelezinho wasn't at the hospital when I went there to look her up, so I sat and had midmorning tea and cookies with two kindly, radiant old Irish women in brown Franciscan habits, Sister Olive and Sister Maeve. Sister Maeve had put in fifty-one years in Uganda. "I've seen the country come up and go down," she said. We talked about sex. "It's impossible to tell how many break the Ten Commandments," Sister Olive told me. "Only the recording angel up there knows the tally." "For many years sex was the only outlet in Uganda," Sister Maeve said. "The people were trapped in their homes. There were no social amenities. They lived in fear for years. All those in their twenties know nothing but violence." This was also Widy-Wirski's impression, that there was a lot of sex because there was nothing else to do, no TV, no electricity, no movies. Sister Olive blamed the women. "If the women were monogomous the men would be. They are the ones who give themselves."

From the courtyard came the same ululating shrieks I had heard in the church in Kinshasa and in the street below my hotel in Nairobi. This time they were from a woman who Sister Maeve said was "off her top" and hung out at the hospital. "There she goes again."

A woman who had just come from Germany to work in the

leprosy hospital at Buluba joined us. We talked about how the AIDS victims have become a new category of pariah, of untouchables, the way lepers used to be. She said if she saw any AIDS she'd jump right into it, she'd treat the pruritic skin rash with Whitfield ointment, the opportunistic infections with potassium permanganate. She had worked in another rural hospital in Uganda several years before, but she couldn't say whether there was any AIDS then because nobody was looking for it, and "as with most diseases you don't diagnose unless you're aware that the disease exists." She told me that there had been a lot of leprosy in Europe two hundred years ago, then it had mysteriously disappeared. "Wouldn't it be marvelous if AIDS did the same, if it just went away, mutated out of existence, went back wherever it came from?" I asked. "Yes, it would be great," Widy-Wirski said when I was talking to him about this later, "because I can't foresee any medical treatment."

I went to Mulago Hospital, where a report widely disseminated in the West said that "twenty-seven percent of those admitted" were seropositive. A young intern showed me around one of the general medical wards, where at the moment there were four AIDS patients. They had the usual symptoms: diarrhea, weight loss, oral thrush, skin rash. We visited with Patient M., eighteen, admitted a few days before with an eight-month history of fever and diarrhea. The girl managed a smile from her bed. She didn't speak English. "She doesn't know she has AIDS although we have told her mother," the intern said. "Sometimes when you tell the patients they tend to take it badly. Three doctors here have died of AIDS. One committed suicide. The doctor who committed suicide had had a girlfriend who died of AIDS."

The ward, one of four with AIDS patients in the hospital, was getting about twenty new cases a month. "When we see the patient is too far gone, we don't admit him," the intern went on. "This one's a bit better than when she came. We've been giving her IV fluids, blood transfusions, and antibiotics. She was a high school student and she got pregnant, so she stopped her studies. She was staying with her parents and had a good number of boyfriends. Definitely more than one partner a week, in a period of two weeks at least four. Just from friendship. We don't usually get full-time harlots." We moved on. Patient M. raised a long-fingered hand and waved goodbye feebly.

Twenty-two-year-old Patient N., from a suburb of Kampala, was still beautiful and had big sunken pleading eyes. She was admitted with a three-month history of fever, diarrhea, and abdominal pain. Her hefty sister was at her bedside. The patient was a widow. Her husband was shot by Obote's men in 1985. A civilian, he was a peasant farmer in the central Buganda region. "Just killed anyhow," the intern told me. "They were married three years and had two children. The oldest is three and a half. A man was helping her look after her children before the fever started. While her husband was alive there were no others but then there was someone else, only one. They separated because of her illness, but he is all right." So in the last five years she'd had only two men? "No. More than two. But she doesn't know where they are." How many then? "Around six."

Widy-Wirski had told me, "Here you ask them their contacts and they tell you two-five-ten. In the Central African Republic they'll tell you a hundred. They're just more modest here."

IN THE MORNING I confirm my flight to Rome with Uganda Airlines. The girl at the ticket window, after hearing my reason for being in the country, says mischievously, "I hope you're not working too hard on zero grazing yourself." Then she grows serious and asks, "Are we really the worstest?"

A little while later I am picked up in a Land-Rover by

Edward, my driver, and Baker, the mechanic. We head south to Masaka and Rakai, the areas of heavy infestation. The morning rains have made the road slick. We pass an overturned truck. Free bananas. The rusted wreck of one of Obote's tanks. A roadblock. "So many were killed at this roadblock," Edward tells me. In 1986, guerrillas from Museveni's National Resistance Army came out of the bush and liberated Masaka, then they marched into Kampala. A woman from there told me that "when the soldiers reached the capital they slept with almost all the women, even married women, they had been without so long. Many women were waiting for them because compared to the last government they were very handsome and kind."

The Land-Rover stalls out. "Water has entered the coil," Baker informs me after looking under the hood. With the help of my trusty Swiss Army knife he clears up the problem. We continue past fuming mud pyramids in which homemade bricks are curing and pull into Masaka, a crumbling gutted ruin of a city. It was reduced to rubble during the Uganda-Tanzania war of 1978–79, when Idi Amin was overthrown, and again during its liberation by Obote. It looks as if it had been hit by an earthquake.

We arrive at St. Joseph's Hospital, a few miles out of town, run by the Medical Missionaries of Mary. A sampling of a hundred outpatients here found thirty percent of them seropositive. A dozen young women are sitting on benches waiting to be examined, giving off the familiar smell of diarrhea, of AIDS. Okware told me to look up Sister O'Brien. While I wait for her in the refectory, a nun tells me that the hospital was cut off for four months in 1985–86, during the most recent war of liberation. "We treated lorryloads of NRA casualties. AIDS was not yet a problem. But no sooner was the war over than it became one."

Sister O'Brien is a fiery, feisty old Irishwoman. She interviewed me: What are you doing here? Where's your letter of authorization? Don't have one. Well, I can't help you then. And who's this? Baker identifies himself impressively as my "transportation officer." At last she relents. She gives me a few minutes but talking to patients is out of the question and there will be no numbers—those I have to get from Okware.

"We're a general hospital," she says. "Malaria, sickle-cell anemia, and tuberculosis have historically been the main problems. We first noticed AIDS in 1983. It was obvious what we were dealing with. There was a dramatic change in the disease pattern. It was the postwar era, and there was a lot of malnutrition. Malaria, tuberculosis, and typhoid were on the rise. This was to be expected. But then we began to see wasting and fulminating diarrhea. It first appeared among raiders going across Lake Victoria and running around with women all over the place, through swamps, picking up diseases. But then we began to see babies being born with it. We knew that we were dealing with something new, and we knew from reading the British medical journals what it was—AIDS."

Why did it break out here? I ask Sister O'Brien. "Anywhere there is an army there is disease," she tells me. "People are moving about and malnourished and there is a lot of venereal disease, which predisposes them to AIDS.

"Until 1974 there was a good health service in Uganda, with an education program and a nationwide disease surveillance system that was the best in Africa," Sister O'Brien continues, "but now the Masaka and Rakai hospitals are not functioning very well, and we are getting their patients." I ask how many the hospital is getting a month. She says to ask Okware. "Recently many of the patients are going back to the traditional healers because of the helplessness of Western medicine," she continues. "We can only tide someone over the acute phase."

WE HEAD SOUTH into the Rakai district. There is no hospital in this part of Rakai, only the Kalisizo Health Center. The head of the center is Dr. Folgencius Mwebe, a small, keenly intelligent man with a large head who is very nervous about my not having a letter of authorization. Everyone is worried that he or she will be blamed for saying things that lead to sensational reports like the *Reader's Digest*'s one about the "whole villages being decimated." (In fact in some villages on the Tanzanian border where hardly anyone is left alive, the word "decimated" in its original Latin sense—that one-tenth of the population has been destroyed—is probably an understatement.)

This time by sheer luck the district administrator happens to show up and gives Mwebe permission to talk. Mwebe tells me he thought the disease had already appeared by 1980. One of his uncles died of Kaposi's that year, and last year his uncle's wife and one of his girlfriends died of "classical AIDS immunosuppression." Four of his friends got sick and killed themselves: two by hanging, one by swallowing rat poison, and one by electrocuting himself.

Mwebe is also treating AIDS at a private clinic down the road. He uses disposable needles (and then disposes of them) and puts on a new pair of rubber gloves for each patient. "We discourage very many AIDS patients at the center," he tells me, "because there are no beds or food for them. We give them medicine and send them back home unless there is an emergency, such as if they have pneumonia. If they come in the first stages and we are not sure they have it, we take their blood and send it to Kitovo for an ELISA. Many are staying home because they know the hospitals can do nothing and are going to the traditional healers for their fever or diarrhea."

He takes me to see one of the healers, who lives about a mile from the village in a reed-fenced compound of spiked thatch huts. She is a faith healer who is just starting out.

We enter one of the huts, and Mwebe gives a ritual greeting to the people inside and they return it. The greetings are exchanged in a high hum as if they were a mantra being uttered or a rosary being told. "*Irade*. You're welcome," the greeting goes. "How was your day?" Traditional welcome offerings of dried coffee beans and halved calabashes full of *mwegne muganda*, Ugandan banana beer, are passed to Mwebe, Baker, Edward, and me. The head man, two elders, and three women are sitting around on rush mats. One of the old men passes me an oil lamp, a flaming wick in a tin can, so I can see to write. The chief's daughter, Mary Caroline, is the healer. She is thirty-two, a hefty woman pregnant with her third child. I have to rely on Mwebe for an English précis of what she says. "Her belief is that she heals by the power of God," Mwebe explains. "She believes that Slim is not an infection from a virus, but some false spirits or wrong air which infects people who have done wrong. Even if a patient has no symptoms she can see he will get them, so she asks his guardian spirits to come and send the bad spirits away. She is in the mood to receive your spirits now." Mary Caroline begins to sway. "Our angels are talking," she says. She sees my seven "elders" behind me. She can name them. Kazeroni, Zebroni, Capriolani . . . Zaceri. I tell her she is right. I do have an ancestor named Zachary. "This is modern healing," Mwebe says, "through Holy Mary and Jesus. Everybody can be treated, even a white man." When we get up to go, ritual leave-takings are hummed around the hut. Pray for me and I'll pray for you. "Your three other elders refused to talk," Mary Caroline tells me.

From there we go to see a woman who is staying home to die, passing on the way the grave of a recent AIDS victim. The woman is the second of four wives of a banana businessman who died a few months ago. "I've been treating her for a rash and oral thrush for about a year," Mwebe says. "Her brother died also. He had dementia and bit his mother's finger off when she was feeding him. Her daughter was my housekeeper." We park and get out. "This is my village," Mwebe says, "I live three houses over." There are drums in the darkness from a drinking place behind a banana grove. We enter the hut. Again the high hummed greetings. The patient is thirty years old and still strong, a fine-looking woman. We sit with her in the Land-Rover so we can talk privately. Mwebe asks her a lot of questions in Luganda. "She's been in intensive treatment several times but she's in remission now," he says. "She has a cold two weeks old that has been giving her a lot of chest pain, and a noisy abdomen but no more diarrhea. She has flatulence and a bit of vomiting. Three months ago she had generalized pruritis, itching of the skin and vulva from the fungus that affects immunocompromised people. She hasn't gone to a healer but she uses some herbs herself. There is no money to pay for medicine. The public clinics are free but they have no drugs.

"Her biggest problem is that she can't work, and she has two children at school. She had left her father's home and now she has had to come back to be looked after like a child. She knows she has it. On and off I have been talking to her. She accepts it and waits."

We get out of the Land-Rover and I give her a crumpled bank note for medicine so she can stave off the inevitable a little longer. She drops to the ground. I think she has collapsed, then I realize she has given me a deep curtsy of gratitude.

SINCE THERE IS nowhere to stay in Kalisozo, we drive back up to Masaka. All the hotels are full, and we wander up and down through vermin-infested back alleys knocking on the doors of roach-infested hostelries. There is not a room to be had, but at last we find a place for me to sleep, a windowless basement pleasure dome with gaudy furniture and mirrors, probably the scene of a lot of transmission. "We get you one tonight?" the

man at the desk asks. No, thanks. No way, José. Baker and
Edward say they will crash with local contacts. Then we go to
scare up something to eat. The only place still open is a bar.
We wash down chapatis with Bell beer. This is the most de-
generate scene, the closest thing to Sodom I had ever seen.
Guys, completely bombed, with girls on their laps, etc. Obviously nobody cares about getting AIDS.

Back in my pleasure dome I curl up with an essay on
Uganda's troubled history, Eustace Gashigu's "Towards Peace
in Uganda." I learn from it that intertribal warfare in Uganda
had been going on with few interruptions since at least 1570,
when the dominant king of the region was called Rubagirama-
sega, which meant "he who butchers humans for vultures." In
1919 a remarkable Queen Muhumuz "collided with the British
government" and promised to provide her followers with supernatural powers that would render them immune to bullets, just
as Alice Lakwena, the leader of the Holy Spirit guerrilla movement, is now promising her followers.

According to Gashigu, the recent troubles in Rakai date
to 1972, when guerrillas based in Tanzania were already trying
to overthrow Amin. There was raping and pillaging on both sides
of the border. Gashigu laments not only the "dehumanizing and
horrendous things we have done to one another," but remarks
that the vegetation in urban areas and by the roadsides "largely
looks miserable," and that "some individuals have even speculated that the recent unexpected and inconvenient shifts in
Uganda's traditional weather patterns were somehow connected
with the country's local and national unrest."

I have breakfast with a Zaïrois *commerçant* from Butembo,
a sunny, friendly town also right on the equator, with a distant
view of the Ruwenzori Mountains. The SIDA situation there, he
said, was *"pas grave."* I ask if he slept with anybody here. He
says, "No. These days it is best to remain *célibataire.*"

We are on the road by seven-thirty, headed south toward Kasensero. A few hours later we are driving through a swampy low country that looks just like the Pantanal do Mato Grosso, Brazil. Amazing. The heart of Africa and the heart of South America are just the same. White mushrooms that look like the hallucinogenic genus *Psilocybc* have sprouted in the cow paddies. We come to the edge of a spectacular scarp, a milky white ocean spread out before us into distant haze. Lake Victoria. Two fish eagles, with snow white bodies and extended brown wings, are teetering on the updraft. The forest below is loud with birds. Two miles off, on the lake shore, a cluster of zinc-roofed shacks catches the sun. Kasensero. Stop, I told Edward, this is beautiful. I walk to the edge of the road to pee. There is something big and black and shiny coiled in the tall grass right in front of me, two feet away. Yoiks! A spitting cobra. I jump back. The snake doesn't slither off as much as deliquesce into the grass.

The road down the scarp is little better than a rock slide. We meet some of the smugglers coming up it in a truck loaded with sheets of roofing that they tell us they bought in Tanzania for a thousand bob apiece and are planning to sell in Masaka for fifteen hundred. "When are you going to bring the medicine?" one of them asks. "We are dying." "There is no medicine yet," I say, "but we are working on it."

We reach the village, two rows of mud and wattle shacks right on the water, in the middle of absolutely nowhere. The smugglers are unloading two graceful thirty-foot open boats with huge outboards. Mattresses. Crates of pencils from the People's Republic of China. Drinking glasses from Dar-es Salaam. I am taken to the office of David Bijga, who is at a table, entering the cargo in a Traders' Association logbook. He is a customs man. The ministry of finance got wind of the smugglers' operation—Slim blew their cover—and wanted a piece of the action, so it sent Bijga down a couple of months ago. Now the smugglers are legit. They are traders. They pay duty.

Bijga says there are about a hundred people in the village and he doesn't know if anybody has Slim. He sends for someone who knew those who are sick. Soon a young man—one of the traders—appears. I buy a round of warm beer. It is very hot in the shed and thick with flies. My skin is red and raw. I can't wait to get out of here. The trader says, "There are ten with Slim now, and those who have died are a hundred and twenty. It came through sex with girls in Tanzania, but not only Tanzanian girls, ones from Zambia and Zimbabwe. In Tanzania there is a lot of Slim, same as here. [The adjacent Kagera region of northern Tanzania seems to have as serious an epidemic of AIDS as the one in Rakai. According to the Tanzanians, the disease was brought in by fishermen who had crossed the border and slept with the girls in Rakai. Their name for it is Juliana, after a fabric that was the rage with Baganda women a few years back.] The sick ones here say the people of Ukerewe and Kome [islands in the Tanzanian port of Lake Victoria] did it to them. The people on the islands have had Slim from the beginning. It came from there."

I wonder if it is worth taking a boat to Ukerewe and Kome and decide against it. This is far enough for me. Some more enterprising quester can chase the elusive source over the next rise.

NAPLES

My balcony at the grand, *fin-de-siècle* Hotel Vesuvio looks out on the Castell' dell' Ovo, a lozenge-shaped citadel sloshed by the cobalt waters of the highly polluted and dying Mediterranean. At various points in its long history the castle has been a monastery, a fortress, or a prison, depending on the need at hand. Now it is a conference center. Six hundred people, among them some of the most prominent names in AIDS research, have come

198 | AFRICAN MADNESS

here for the Third International Symposium on AIDS and Related Cancers in Africa. Naples is an appropriate place for such a conference not only because it was here that syphilis, the last great sexually transmitted pandemic, first appeared in the West five centuries ago, but because in its seething squalor and infant-mortality rate—the highest on the continent—it is more like an African city than a European one. There is also the provocative proximity of Pompeii, where an earlier sex-positive society was wiped out—only by a volcano, not a virus. Now a ruin twenty minutes by train down the coast, two thousand years ago Pompeii was a flourishing Roman port with about twenty thousand in-habitants, roughly the size of Lyantonde, a trading center along the international highway west of Masaka, where local girls wait in bars to meet the long-distance drivers, and incredibly high infection rates have been reported. In A.D. 79, in the midst of all the fun, the earth's African plate rammed up against the Italian peninsula, and an avalanche of glowing magma spewed forth from nearby Vesuvius. Within hours Pompeii was smothered.

I spend the morning at Pompeii the day before the symposium gets rolling—take in the biphallic fresco of Priapus, the Roman god of sexual abandon, and the couple turned to stone *in flagrante delicto*—and get back to Naples in time for lunch at a waterfront restaurant with two brothers from Newport Beach who are exploring markets for a Chinese herbal immunostimulant that has been used to treat cancer for centuries. Capitalism at work. "We're here to scope out the problem," one of them explains. "We've got to do the preclinical efficacy and toxicology work. We'll probably market it in the Third World rather than the First. Dealing with the FDA is a pain in the ass." So you're focusing on the role of the immunosuppression rather than on the virus, I ask. "What does AIDS stand for?" the other brother retorts.

Drug companies and the purveyors of AIDS paraphernalia

have established a modest promotional presence at the conference, and as the participants drift in from various corners of the
globe they are issued green tote bags from Wellcome Diagnos-
tics, the producers of one of the most widely used ELISA tests.
The tote bags contain abstracts of the scientific papers to be
presented, note pads, and little pens stamped with the company's
logo, all of which are useful for sorting out what is going on and
which events to attend. There are so many offerings, so many
elegant slide presentations, so much to take in. But I keep seeing
the hurt, hopeless look of the patient at the Hospital Simão
Mendes; the deep curtsy of the woman with AIDS in Rakai. I
keep smelling diarrhea and hearing the smuggler ask, "Where's
the medicine?" Despite the efforts of all these scientists, four
million Africans are going to die. Or is it six?

This kind of thinking, of course, isn't going to get anybody
anywhere. "We may as well stop working if that's the attitude,"
Dani Bolognese says to me. Bolognese is a virologist and the
head of the AIDS program at Duke. He's "shotgunning" three
or four vaccine approaches with Gallo. "We're gonna get this
one. We're gonna lick it. It's going to be tough, but you take
your balls in your hands and go for it."

The problems preventing AIDS from being licked take up
most of the symposium. There are panels on the urgent need
for a rapid blood test, on the problems of false positives and
false negatives, on what is meant by the growing numbers of
Africans who are testing positive for both HIV-1 and HIV-2, on
the alarming rise in perinatal transmission, and on the results
of new surveys that reveal even higher levels of infection than
had been suspected before.

One question that isn't discussed formally is that of the "origin" of AIDS—partly because this is a politically sensitive
question, and there are a lot of African participants, partly because most scientists regard it as a beginner's question, an un-

productive can of worms. As Jonathan Mann, the director of the
World Health Organization's global AIDS program, remarks, "The
retroviral map is like a map of the world in the fourteenth century. Some coastline is well defined, other portions are blank and
infested with dragons. The picture is still much too fragmentary
to draw any conclusions." He thinks AIDS-like viruses may have
been epidemic for a long time. "There is a preconception that
they came from Africa, but the data is relatively slim. Let's wait
and see." This is what Luc Montagnier thinks. "Maybe we should
be looking in another part of the world," he tells a group of journalists who have been grilling him on the African origin question.

To Mann and other scientists the important thing now is
not where the epidemic started but how it spreads. "Every era
has the disease of its time," Mann says. "Plague and syphilis
arose from the opening of trade routes with Asia and the Americas and the sudden contact of parts of the world that had never
been in contact before. This is the global village disease." To
the Western man in the street, however, the question of the
African origin of AIDS is important because he has been told
that it's only a matter of time until the pattern of AIDS in the
U.S. and Europe becomes "African."

Such a scenario seems unlikely. Africa is not the West.
Virtually the entire African population is immunosuppressed.
Many sexually active Africans have untreated venereal diseases.
Most of the blood supply is not screened. Unsterilizable plastic
syringes are used over and over. Most Africans are illiterate, so
it's hard to reach those at risk and to convince them that they
must change their ways. Much of the region is in turmoil. Health
services are woefully inadequate for the burgeoning urban populations. So what is there, one wonders, to keep AIDS from
spreading until every African between the ages of fifteen and
forty-five gets it? Our gays, on the other hand, are educable.
Many have already altered their sexual behavior, reined in dra-

matically. Plus they do not by and large sleep with women, so they are not going to give AIDS to the general population. Perhaps the only part of the West that Africa might serve as a model for is the IV drug population in the inner city.

A FEW DAYS later, as I sat with Quinn and Bolognese on the plane to New York, I thought about the unprecedented merging and mixing and growing together of the world's population that has taken place in the past few decades, the tremendous release of people from their traditional confines, the enormous flow from the villages to the cities of the Third World, and from the cities of the Third World to the immigrant outskirts of New York, London, Paris, Rome, Cologne, Marseilles. I thought of how HIV must have become airborne—airplane-borne—traveling slipstreams from continent to continent: tens of thousands of revelers flying down to Rio for Carnaval, for instance. Now Brazil, one of the world's most mixed societies, faces an epidemic potentially as devastating as Africa's.

I imagined this archetypical communicable disease traveling along the mutually manipulative interface of the First and Third Worlds in countless copulations, and like a swallowed dye pill illuminating all the *liaisons dangereuses*, the thousands upon thousands of illicit premarital, extramarital, interracial, and homosexual encounters that must have taken place for it to spread as far as it has. I thought of how it is just hitting India, Taiwan, Japan, the Philippines, how seventy-five percent of the hemophiliacs in Denmark were contaminated by unscreened blood that came from the U.S. several years ago, how one out of five men in the South Bronx are now infected and four in five of the heroin addicts in a Catholic rehabilitation center outside Milan, how girls from Mombasa are taking the virus up the east coast of Africa to Addis Ababa, one of the world centers of prostitution, a sexual mecca for Arab men, so it is only a matter of time before the disease spreads into the Arab world, where the predilection for buggery will provide a brisk amplification system, how the twenty-five thousand Eskimos in the Northwest territories—another legendary sex-positive culture—are bracing for the arrival of the disease. Education efforts are hampered by the absence of a word for AIDS in Inuktituk, their lingua franca. The closest thing is *qupiqqiqtaaniq tuqqunnaqtumik aaqqiktaujunnangitumik aaokkuungayoommik*, which means the disease in the blood that cannot be cured and can kill you.

It struck me that for a microcosm of the melting pot process one had to look no further than this completely booked and wait-listed Rome–New York Jumbo 747. Among the four hundred passengers winging their way to the great land whose politically admirable but epidemiologically lamentable motto is E Pluribus Unum were Indians and Arabs, Venezuelans, Poles, Africans, Israelis, Italians, Turks, and Bulgarians, not to mention Americans of assorted hues and stripes—a rich cross-section of the human cornucopia. Quinn said that statistically three people aboard the plane ought to be carrying the virus.